The Contemporary Cottage Garden

The Contemporary Cottage Garden

CLIMATE-FRIENDLY, MINDFUL METHODS FOR GROWING FLOWERS AND FOOD

Pamela Hubbard

Photography by Rob Cardillo

TIMBER PRESS
PORTLAND, OREGON

Photo and illustration credits appear on page 243.

Timber Press
Workman Publishing
Hachette Book Group, Inc.
1290 Avenue of the Americas
New York, New York 10104
timberpress.com

Timber Press is an imprint of Workman Publishing,
a division of Hachette Book Group, Inc.
The Timber Press name and logo are registered
trademarks of Hachette Book Group, Inc.
Printed in Dongguan, China (TLF), on responsibly
sourced paper.
Text and cover design by Catherine Casalino

ISBN 978-1-64326-375-5
A catalog record for this book is available
from the Library of Congress.

To my children, Mark and Maria, who convinced me to write this book; to my four amazing grandchildren, Harrison, Jonathan—who loves to garden, Anthony, and Mateo; and to my husband, Duane, for his love and unwavering support

Contents

As a child, I believed the pretty Erysimum *that my grandmother, Ethel Gilliver, called gillyflower was named for her.*

Preface

When I was a little girl in England, I thought *Erysimum*, which some call wallflower and my grandmother called gillyflower, was named for her, not only because it was her favorite of all the blooms in her pretty cottage garden, but also because Grandmother's name, before marriage, was Ethel Gilliver. My tiny ears heard Ethel Gilliflower, increasing my admiration for her. I assimilated a great deal of horticultural lore from shadowing my grandmother as she planted, weeded, and watered, and I acquired a lifelong love for the seemingly uncontrived beauty of the cottage garden. When I moved to the Pocono Mountains of Pennsylvania, I dreamed of creating a garden just like hers.

The world has changed enormously since those halcyon days spent in my grandmother's garden. Global issues such as an increasingly erratic environment with unpredictable weather events frustrate everyone—especially the gardener. My garden began as a traditional cottage garden modeled upon my grandmother's. It developed, however, into an avenue for solving some of the environmental and social problems we face today.

I discovered the extraordinary problem-solving potential of cottage gardens when working with new clients as a garden coach. I always inquire, "What is your favorite garden style?" Frequently, they say, "The cottage garden." When I ask, "What is your greatest challenge?" they give me a different answer today than home gardeners gave ten or fifteen years ago. Previously, they complained about rocky soil or deer damage, as both are prevalent in the Pocono Mountains. Nowadays, they are more likely to say, "Unpredictable weather events," or "I want flowers but have to grow veggies because of rising food prices." A client shared with me the stresses of caring for her mother, who is suffering from Alzheimer's disease. She said, "I prefer cottage gardens, but I've been advised that a therapeutic garden may help my mother." I can reassure each client that their desire for a traditional cottage garden and these modern-day problems are not mutually exclusive.

My garden began as a traditional English-style cottage garden but became much more.

My cottage garden taught me it is possible to create a beautiful space that helps solve some of the pressing problems of the day.

Now I show my clients how to install a cottage garden–style rain garden or gravel garden to solve wet weather or drought challenges. I explain that the original cottage garden had vegetables planted among the flowers. Attractive vegetable plants such as Swiss chard and herbs like dill add beauty and practicality to a cottage garden flower bed. I reveal the charm of the cottage garden as a healing garden or a sensory space for the client caring for her mother. Healing and sensory gardens benefit the patient and relieve the caregiver's stress.

This book not only enables the home gardener to realize their dream of creating a cottage garden, but also covers these and many other pressing problems with practical advice and step-by-step instructions. The book explains how the cottage gardener, in their small way, can successfully tackle more extensive issues, such as changing weather and stressful living. The result is a cottage garden with traditional elements and a nontraditional focus—a resource in this ever-changing world.

Introduction: Getting the Most from This Book

Cottage gardens are dearly beloved by many. My goal is to provide a clear guide to creating an English-style cottage garden while explaining how even novice home gardeners can, in their small way, effectively manage current global concerns, such as extreme weather events.

The book has two parts: The first details the cottage garden's historical evolution and distinctive elements. Born in England in the fourteenth century, the cottage garden has evolved into a diverse mixture of the gardener's favorite plants. Features include wide and curvy borders, a riot of color, many potted plants, and often a fence for an enclosure. There is little or no lawn. Instead, meandering paths between planted areas, with plants growing in the cracks between rocks and gravel, provide beauty and serenity. The section shows how the gardener can reflect the flavor of an English garden with plants appropriate to their area conditions.

In my cottage-style garden, I grow plants that evoke memories of my English heritage, such as crocosmia (*Crocosmia* ×*curtonus* 'Lucifer'), which my mother called montbretia. It was one of her favorite flowers. I try to grow my grandmother's gillyflower (*Erysimum cheiri*), but it dislikes the Poconos' climate. I have some success with the western wallflower (*Erysimum capitatum*) that is native to North America. I have English bluebells (*Hyacinthoides non-scripta*) in my garden. As a little girl, I would gather bluebells from the nearby woods—a bunch for my mother and one for my teacher. In my Pocono garden, I also have a David Austin rose called 'Lichfield Angel' that brings back happy memories of my weekly visits to Lichfield Cathedral in my

An early crop of rhubarb, snow peas, and cabbage harvested from my kitchen garden for sharing.

high school years. I attended high school in Lichfield, England, and loved the nearby cathedral. The Lichfield Angel, discovered in the cathedral's basement in 2003, is a remarkable survival of early medieval sculpture made of carved limestone. After its discovery, I returned to Lichfield from the United States to see it and bought a picture to display in my home. David Austin named a new rose, the 'Lichfield Angel', for the sculpture.

I make new memories as I garden with my grandchildren. I taught Jonathan how to make miniature gardens in tubs and repurposed containers. He made some to display in my cottage garden. Although he is an adult now, he maintains and refurbishes them annually.

The first section then defines the global problems facing us today: pollution of our planet, extreme weather, rising food prices, the changing workplace, international conflict, and more significant stress, illness, and isolation—exacerbated by the COVID-19 pandemic. The book explains how these problems affect the home gardener directly.

The book's second part provides clear, doable solutions to the problems, beginning with pollution. Step-by-step instructions propel the reader into workable remedies for home gardening. The book shows why sustainable gardening is crucial and how to implement organic methods. It also addresses making and using compost, attracting pollinators, and dealing with invasive species. You will learn how to keep your garden healthy without using toxic chemicals. A flourishing and thriving cottage garden will be the beautiful result.

We know that as we pollute our planet, global warming occurs. My area in the eastern United States is experiencing unpredictable weather events. I show how I incorporated a rain garden that blends into the cottage garden style and a gravel garden with a cottage garden flair, including a list of suitable plantings for each scenario. In addition, the book enumerates other practical suggestions for achieving success despite climate challenges.

*Cottage garden flowers, such as lupine (*Lupinus*) and catmint (*Nepeta*), add to a feeling of peace in the healing garden.*

Because of rising food prices, personal budgets, and problems of availability and distribution, more gardeners are growing their own vegetables and herbs. In an English-style cottage garden, vegetables are often grown among the flowers. I show how to do this with companion plantings and other tips, and I discuss sharing the harvest with those who are food insecure.

Since the COVID-19 pandemic, people continue to work at home. Fresh flowers on the work desk brighten the room and lift spirits during long stretches of isolation. However, bringing profuse bouquets into the house means a limited show in the garden—solve this problem by creating a cutting garden. The book provides instructions for growing, maintaining, and harvesting flowers for cutting.

Some gardeners may care for a family member who is seriously ill or in crisis, for example, with PTSD. For those caregivers, the book shows how to create a healing garden that perfectly fits the cottage garden style. Incorporating water, sound, and lighting, I discuss appropriate plants and how to reduce maintenance. We would all benefit from our own healing garden, bringing nature's positive effects to our physical and mental well-being. Therefore, I will show the beautiful one I created at my home.

New gardeners soon discover gardening is an excellent stress reliever in these challenging times. For those who have not yet started gardening, the book enumerates the many benefits, with extensive detail on creating a cottage garden that is also a sensory garden—the perfect stress reliever. Sensory gardens are suitable for small or large spaces. They may be designed for just one sense, such as a fragrance garden, or all five senses. Sensory gardens make perfect children's gardens.

This book will prepare future generations to deal with climate and environmental issues. Adults can use it as a guidebook to instill in their youth numerous strategies for recognizing gardens and gardening as a practical and beautiful resource.

In a world of uncertainty, gardening can ground us. By looking at a familiar garden design from the past and bringing it up to date, we can feel a continuity with a more peaceful time. This book will encourage and instruct new gardeners and inspire more experienced gardeners to delve further into the characteristics and benefits of cottage garden style in this time of unprecedented environmental and societal change.

A picture of the Lichfield Angel, found in Lichfield Cathedral, hangs in my home evoking lovely memories.

Meandering paths with plants growing between the rocks or gravel are a charming element of the cottage garden style.

I grow Crocosmia *'Lucifer' because it was one of my mother's favorite flowers.*

David Austin's rose 'Lichfield Angel' brings back happy memories of time spent in Lichfield Cathedral, England, in my youth.

My grandson Jonathan made his first miniature garden when he was seven years old.

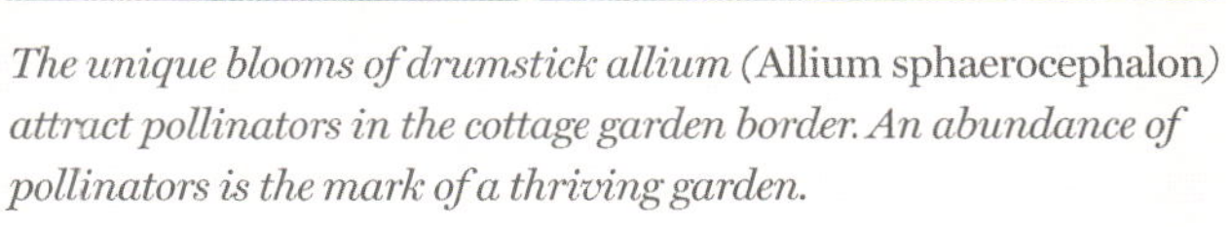

*The unique blooms of drumstick allium (*Allium sphaerocephalon*) attract pollinators in the cottage garden border. An abundance of pollinators is the mark of a thriving garden.*

PART I

THE COTTAGE GARDEN THEN AND NOW

A path for strolling through the garden at Grafton Cottage in England.

CHAPTER 1

The Time-Honored Garden

The cottage garden; most for use design'd,
Yet not of beauty destitute.
—CHARLOTTE SMITH

As a history major, I've found that understanding a modern-day phenomenon is often easier when placed in historical context. So, we will journey to a typical cottage garden in England and delve into its rich historical background. Following this brief introduction to the roots of cottage gardening, I discuss the elements of an English cottage garden. Then I provide a clear plan for creating a beautiful flower bed in the cottage garden style. Yes, you may start digging immediately and not wait until the end of this book to own a lovely cottage garden. I'll guide you all the way, including an introduction to my two goats, Doodles and Petunia. Livestock in the cottage garden was a typical element in the past but, I assure you, an optional element for today's gardener.

The English Cottage Garden

As I stroll through a cottage garden in England during one of my frequent visits from the United States, I delight in the glorious colors and varied textures of an abundance of flowers covered with butterflies and bees. Despite the challenges of an unstable climate, the English cottage garden still maintains its traditional beauty.

I wonder, however, what I would see if I had a time machine to take me to the cottage garden at its inception. I would find myself in a very different setting. I would see few flowers, just vegetables growing haphazardly, with chickens and pigs foraging among the utilitarian plan.

Like the peasants of 1350, I grow cabbages in my cottage garden.

THE FIRST ENGLISH COTTAGE GARDENS

Peasants created the first cottage gardens in 1350 following the two-year devastation of the Black Death pandemic. This squalid disease, caused by the bacterium *Yersinia pestis*, raged across the Eastern Hemisphere, killing one-third of the population. Although it is similar to the comparatively recent COVID-19 pandemic in terms of societal impact, the Black Death had much higher infection and mortality rates. Finding themselves with a decimated workforce, landowners gave cottages and land to surviving peasants in exchange for free labor.

The peasants' cottages were hovels with wattle and daub walls (interwoven sticks and branches daubed with animal dung combined with wet clay, soil, and straw) and leaky roofs thatched with straw. They raised plants and animals for food. Their pigs and chickens wandered around the gardens in summer and lived with them inside the cottage in winter. The peasants ate little meat; their main meal was pottage, a dish of vegetables in stock or water seasoned with herbs. They planted vegetables and herbs haphazardly in every available space, with no design as we know it. They produced beans, cabbages, fennel, leeks, onions, peas, and turnips. They harvested fruit, such as blackberries and raspberries, from the hedgerows, transplanting them into their gardens as the Middle Ages drew to a close. Still, the cottage garden showed little change until the sixteenth century.

The pretty primula, introduced to England by the Huguenots in the sixteenth century, brings the beauty of spring to today's cottage garden.

THE DEVELOPMENT OF THE COTTAGE GARDEN TRADITION

The Huguenots, artisan refugees who traveled from Europe to England at the end of the sixteenth century, introduced their best-loved plants, such as the beautiful auricula (*Primula auricula*), one of my favorites. Gardeners hybridized flowers to improve their size and form, and they began to create horticultural societies and clubs. They transformed the English cottage garden tradition from the utilitarian to the showy.

THE INFLUENCE OF GREAT GARDENERS

During the eighteenth century, the prosperous gentry of industrial England was tired of the stressful city life and longed for the serenity of the countryside. At the same time, rather than expansive lawns, man-made lakes, and enormous trees surrounding their homes, the aristocracy turned to the free and easy style of the cottage garden. Four great gardeners firmly established this change: William Robinson (1838–1935), Gertrude Jekyll (1843–1932), Vita Sackville-West (1892–1962), and Christopher Lloyd (1921–2006). They created large-scale gardens, impractical for today's cottage gardeners, but they legitimized cottage garden design. The work of these extraordinary innovators continues to inspire gardeners today.

William Robinson's 1883 book, *The English Flower Garden*, is still helpful for depicting traditional cottage garden plants. Robinson extracted the essential elements from the cottage garden style and focused on the attributes of individual flowers.

Gertrude Jekyll was a designer, writer, and artist who created more than 400 gardens in England and several in America. Her designs differed significantly from the angular, modernist gardens in vogue with aristocrats. She produced large-scale herbaceous borders with a completely casual look.

Robinson and Jekyll greatly influenced Vita Sackville-West, as you can see today when visiting her gardens at Sissinghurst and Hidcote. While very large, these gardens retain the intimacy of authentic cottage gardens.

The great garden writer Christopher Lloyd is best known for his gardens at Great Dixter, where he proved it is possible to attain cottage garden style in any environment. His gardens were forever changing as he

A modern herbaceous border at Dorset House in England is in the style of Jekyll.

The Long Border at Great Dixter, England, looks exuberant and uncontrived.

experimented with plants. Lloyd's work encourages the cottage gardener to step outside the box. Fergus Garrett, head gardener and chief executive of the Great Dixter Charitable Trust, continues Lloyd's work, bringing his unique style to the gardens. I am proud to own a signed copy of Lloyd's book, *The Cottage Garden*, which profoundly influences my gardening efforts.

THE COTTAGE GARDEN TODAY IN ENGLAND AND AMERICA

The peasantry's authentic, utilitarian cottage garden has disappeared in England. However, certain principles are evident in allotments, those tiny parcels of land rented to gardeners by the local government. Gardeners usually grow vegetables and some fruit and may be allowed to keep some chickens. Although they may have some flowers in their allotments, they are more likely to plant them around their houses. Today, the informal medley of blooms grown by English gardeners around their homes defines the English cottage garden style as we know it.

In recent years, gardening has become a trendy American pastime. The COVID-19 pandemic led to an increase in vegetable gardening. At the same time, ecological concerns spurred the reduction of lawn space and the use of native plants to attract pollinators. Many would like to create a cottage garden in the English style but fear an increasingly unstable environment, with unpredictable weather events and more pests, makes it too complicated. I will show how it is possible to adapt to changing conditions without losing the essential

The COVID-19 pandemic increased vegetable gardening in the United States.

elements of the traditional cottage garden. As a result, gardeners can do their part in mitigating the adverse effects of global challenges—one garden at a time.

Design Elements of a Cottage Garden

When I retired after twelve years as a school administrator, the family of some of my students gave me a garden book as a parting gift. They knew I was retiring to realize my dream of making a cottage garden modeled after that of my English grandmother. The book I came to treasure was *English Country Gardens* by Ethne Clarke and Clay Perry. As a garden coach, when describing the elements of a cottage garden to my clients, I frequently quote from the book in which Clarke says, "A cottage garden is above all things a place of uncontrived beauty, easily enjoyed, where labour is well-rewarded and quiet pleasures satisfied." However, it is important to note that careful planning is necessary for the garden's beauty to appear uncontrived.

Although early cottage gardens may have had flowers and vegetables growing side by side, in England, when I was a child, cottage flower gardens were often in the front yard, and vegetables were at the back of the house. Incidentally, the British call their yards the front and back gardens; a "yard" in England is an empty lot or refers to Scotland Yard, a police station. (When we first arrived in the United States from England, my young children coined the expression, "the Yarden," when referring to our garden.) Sadly, with the need for more garage space nowadays, many English families use their front gardens as paved or graveled parking spots.

You may locate your cottage garden in front or back or mix vegetables and flowers in one bed, but keep some standard features to create an uncontrived image of profusion. I have identified ten main components to enable you to achieve this appearance.

1. Dense plantings
2. An informal plan
3. A mixture of plant types
4. Wide, curvy borders
5. A riot of color
6. Potted plants
7. Enclosed space
8. Vertical features
9. Meandering paths
10. Little lawn

I planted swaths of coneflower and bee balm to create a picture of uncontrived beauty.

In addition, I will say a few words about livestock in the cottage garden. After all, those pigs and chickens were as crucial as vegetables in the early cottage garden.

DENSE PLANTINGS

The profuse cottage garden flower bed has no wide spaces between plants. When I show you how to create the garden, you will see enough space between plants to allow air circulation and prevent disease. An advantage of denser planting is that the need for weeding is less likely.

INFORMAL PLAN

With an informal plan, you do not need to worry about placing the tallest plants at the back of the bed, those of medium height in the middle, and low growers at the front. When creating an image of profusion, the height of the plant is irrelevant. Similarly, you don't have to make the design symmetrical. For example, when you add a focal point—and all gardens should have a focal point, such as a water feature, a unique plant, or a statue—place it off-center for a more informal look.

MIXTURE OF PLANT TYPES

The key to the appearance of profusion is plant variety. Choose herbaceous perennials, flowering shrubs, herbs, groundcovers, and bulbs. (Herbaceous perennials have leaves and stems that die down to soil level at the end of the growing season; they return each spring, often for several years.) Plant old-fashioned flowers such as delphinium (*Delphinium* spp.), foxglove (*Digitalis* spp.),

Plant densely in a cottage garden border for fewer weeds and an informal look.

hollyhock (*Alcea* spp.), and rose (*Rosa*). Cottage gardens typically contain some plants for their fragrance, such as lavender. Fill in the gaps with pockets of annuals (plants that live for one growing season only).

WIDE, CURVY BORDERS

The undulating lines of wide, curvy borders are more attractive than straight ones. Incidentally, this classic style is trendy today with the naturalistic planting movement. Naturalistic gardens mimic nature, which has few straight lines. Curvy edges make the garden look more extensive, especially in a small space. Cottage gardens are all about surprise. With an angular design, you see the whole garden at once, whereas curves prompt you to wonder what is around that bend.

RIOT OF COLOR

My cottage garden flowers are a mixture of warm and cool colors. Warm colors are orange, red, and yellow, whereas cool colors are blue, green, pink, and purple. There are no hard and fast rules about placing colors together when creating a cottage garden; in nature, any color can pop up next to another. Your riot of color does not look too overwhelming when you plant colors in waves and repeat them. Add a wave of white flowers to provide rest for the eyes.

POTTED PLANTS

An essential element of cottage garden design is the inclusion of plants in containers. Usually, the plants are annuals, but many perennial flowers are good options. Potted plants are incredibly versatile. You may expand your cottage garden to the patio or terrace. I plant bulbs

A whimsical stone birdbath is the focal point in this profuse flower border.

Old-fashioned roses and foxgloves are charming in Jenny Rose Carey's garden at Northview.

Flower borders with curved edges make a small garden look more expansive.

*A wave of white flowers, such as Shasta daisies (*Leucanthemum ×superbum*), provides rest for the eyes.*

*A cool palette of pink roses and purple clematis (*Clematis*), surrounded by green and yellow plant material, provides a beautiful display of color in Jenny Rose Carey's garden.*

A basket of daffodils and a container of spring blooms welcome visitors in springtime.

Use a potted perennial, such as Heuchera, to fill a space in the border at the end of summer.

I plant daffodils in pots in fall. In spring, when they bloom, I place one of the pots in a basket on the porch.

in pots each fall to get an early start on spring. Also, plants in pots provide color when the cottage garden fades between spring and summer. I use them to fill in gaps that occur toward the end of the season. Use a potted plant as a focal point, or place a container of herbs near the kitchen door.

I grow some perennials especially for containers. I use them to fill spaces in the borders. In fall, I take the perennials out of the pots and overwinter them in an empty bed in the vegetable garden.

ENCLOSED SPACE

A low fence, wall, or hedge enclosing the cottage garden is traditional. As a child in England, I took the gates, walls, and fences surrounding old cottages for granted. They were constructed of local materials, plentiful and cheap, such as brick, stone, wattle, or wood. In my neighborhood, a privet or laurel hedge was a standard enclosure. A weathered picket fence surrounding today's cottage garden is beautiful.

VERTICAL FEATURES

Cottage gardens in England are often relatively small, so gardeners tend to plant vertically and horizontally. They cover walls and fences with vines and hanging baskets. A rose-covered arbor is traditional in England. I use arbors to transition from one area of my garden to another, growing beautiful vines over them. Pergolas and obelisks are other options. There is an extraordinary loveliness about a tall trellis wreathed with roses and clematis.

A weathered fence and gate entice you into the herb garden at Northview.

MEANDERING PATHS

Winding paths, like curvy borders, add a sense of wonder about what is around the bend and invite a stroll through the garden. They often lead to a focal point, like a bench or water feature. Plants, such as dianthus and thymes, grow in cracks between rocks. I planted stonecrop (*Sedum rupestre*) and creeping phlox (*Phlox stolonifera*) between mine. Paths of old bricks, gravel, or grass can be practical yet functional additions to your cottage garden design.

LITTLE LAWN

There is little lawn in the cottage garden, just winding paths between the planted areas. I carved flower beds out of my garden's lawn area, reducing the lawn's size and creating grass pathways between the beds.

In addition to the features mentioned, I like to add beautiful or whimsical accessories, often gifts from loved ones, that draw the eye. I have a rustic stone birdbath, an elegant statue, and a collection of stone hedgehogs. Artifacts like these bring personal expression into your garden and make it your own. I expand on this idea later in the book.

LIVESTOCK IN THE COTTAGE GARDEN

Astolat Farm, where I live and garden, is a crop farm where our farmer grows corn, oats, and other grain; we don't raise animals like pigs or cows. We have two goats, Doodles and Petunia, and, until recently, miniature horses. Livestock was essential for the first cottage gardeners. If you have space to add smaller animals, such as chickens or goats, you will enjoy the benefits of fresh eggs and animal manure as valuable compost. First, check with your local authority to ensure no restrictions exist. If you have free-range chickens, use cloches or other plant protection.

Of course, we cannot allow the goats free range of my gardens or they would eat the flowers. They watch me from behind a fence, waiting for me to throw them some weeds. (Sturdy fencing is a must.) I enjoy being in their company when working in the garden. In addition, the den where I write overlooks the goat pasture so I can take pleasure in their antics from indoors. Goats can be very affectionate and have a great sense of curiosity. They are social animals; you can't have just one alone.

I loved my miniature horses, Dude and Charm, but decided not to replace them when they passed. It is important to remember that all animals require responsibility, commitment, and monetary expense. The goats are ideal for my needs as I age. Choose the animals that are right for you. You may have a dog or cat; even a garden cat makes the perfect addition to any cottage garden. I will not forget Dude and Charm. I made a small memorial garden that I call the Horseshoe Garden.

Doodles and Petunia are delightful residents of Astolat Farm.

Vintage horseshoes in the Horseshoe Garden are a memorial to past miniature horses.

A wire cloche protects plants from chicken damage.

A rose-covered arbor is traditional in a cottage garden in England, such as this one at Grafton Cottage.

A clematis-covered arbor provides the transition between my kitchen garden and the cottage garden.

A short but functional old brick path takes visitors through the garden gate at Grafton Cottage, England.

An aerial view shows where I changed a previous lawn area into a pond and flower beds, creating grassy pathways.

A grassy pathway leads you between the pond and the herbaceous border.

In the Healing Garden, a replica of Allegrain's sculpture depicting Venus bathing adds a feeling of tranquility.

Astolat Farm, April 2024.

Creating Your Cottage Garden

Creating a new garden is an exciting experience—you will always remember your first garden. While the gardens at my home, Astolat Farm, were not my first, I was delighted when I retired and finally had time to install them. My husband, Duane, has lived here all his life, and I feel honored to share this beautiful property. A farmer built the house in 1841 or earlier, and although not an English cottage, the rooms have charming, cottage-like features such as exposed beams. I was fortunate to have a blank slate for my gardens because Duane's mother, a world-renowned dog breeder, had used the area around the house for kennels, not gardens, in her lifetime. I would have loved to create a traditional flower garden at the front of the house, but like most farms of the era, our farmhouse is close to the road.

I hope you make a cottage garden for yourself now that you have read this far. Please do not allow the many challenges facing the gardener today to deter you. That is what this book is about. We will take the problems individually and consider their best solutions, first planning your beautiful new garden step by step.

If you are an inexperienced gardener, start small so regular care will be manageable. You can increase the size when you gain more confidence. Also, the cost will be less of an issue if spread out over time. A flower bed or a border about 3 by 8 feet (1 by 2.4 m) is a good beginning.

I located my first garden where I can see it from my favorite chair indoors. The view brings endless pleasure.

Here is the simple seven-step process:

1. Assess the site.
2. Make a list of plants.
3. Put your plan on paper.
4. Select appropriate plants.
5. Prepare the bed.
6. Plant carefully.
7. Water and mulch.

ASSESS THE SITE

Walk around your yard and decide where to locate your new garden. You could install it next to a fence, where you can see it from a house window, or as a colorful approach to your front door. I knew immediately where I should place my first garden. From my favorite chair in a room we call the Garden Room, I looked out at a scraggy lawn, a dying cedar tree, and some invasive multiflora roses. I desired a better view.

Your cottage garden flowers will appreciate plenty of light, so factor six or more hours of sunlight into your location plan. If your garden has little direct sun, make a shady border or bed containing cottage garden elements, except choose plants for a profusion of textures and leaf colors rather than blooms. Note if there is a problem with water runoff or standing water in your preferred area. If the site slopes, you will arrange the plants in terraces to prevent runoff. If the problem is standing water, you must raise the bed.

It is helpful to know the soil type. Soils may be clay, sandy, or loamy. Touch the soil and roll it in your hands. It is clay if it is easily rolled into a sausage shape and is sticky when wet. Clay often has more nutrients than other soil types and retains water better but may need added compost (such as rotted leaves) to break up the clay and allow air for the plants' roots. Sandy soil feels gritty when you roll it between your finger and thumb and you cannot make it into a sausage shape. It drains quickly after rain or watering but dries out fast and is low in plant nutrients. Sandy soils also benefit from being amended with compost. Loamy soils are the most desirable mixture of clay, sand, and silt.

The best way to ensure your soil is optimal for your new plants is to have it tested. Inexpensive, easy-to-use test kits are available at your local County Cooperative Extension office. Each county in the United States has an Extension office that works closely with university experts to provide research-based home garden information and advice. They can also help with soil tests, free of charge or inexpensively. Find the phone number in the government section of the telephone directory or online. I recommend you purchase a soil test and follow the instructions for collecting and mailing a sample. You will receive information on pH, salt content, lime requirement, and available phosphorus, potassium, and magnesium. Follow the recommendations the Extension office will send you with the test results. Good soil is your best investment to ensure thriving flowers and vegetables.

MAKE A LIST OF PLANTS

Begin your list of cottage garden plants with old-fashioned flowers like peony (*Paeonia*), hollyhock, foxglove, and primrose (*Primula vulgaris*).

Add native plants such as purple coneflower (*Echinacea purpurea*), bee balm (*Monarda didyma*), garden phlox (*Phlox paniculata*), and butterfly weed (*Asclepias tuberosa*).

I grow forget-me-nots because they were another of my mother's favorites.

Use this book, plant books, articles in garden magazines, and plant catalogs to identify other plants. Plant catalogs are a joy to peruse, but be aware that your flowers, in their first year, may not look like those portrayed in the catalog. I mark the pages of books and catalogs with sticky notes to look back at the pictures before narrowing my list.

When creating my cottage garden, I visited local gardens and parks to see what thrives in my area and which plants attracted me the most. Talking with fellow gardeners in the neighborhood can be very informative, and you may return home with some gifted plants.

Plan for constant bloom, fragrance, or attractive foliage when selecting plants. I choose flowers that evoke memories: My mother loved montbretia and forget-me-nots (*Myosotis sylvatica*), and, of course, I sometimes

Foxglove is an old-fashioned cottage garden flower.

Delphinium (Delphinium elatum)

Rose (Rosa)

Bee balm (Monarda *'Marshall's Delight'*)

Black-eyed Susan (Rudbeckia)

Clematis (Clematis *'Tie Dye'*)

Garden phlox

Daylily (Hemerocallis *'Siloam Bo Peep'*)

COTTAGE GARDEN FLOWERS

At the garden center, choose plants with vigorous growth.

plant my grandmother's favorite gillyflowers, although they are short-lived annuals in my garden.

Add essential details to your list, including the height and width of the plant, the color of its flowers and leaves, its horticultural name, common names, and hardiness zone. Horticultural names are essential because several plants have the same common name. Remember to check the zone in which each plant grows. You will need to know the hardiness zone for your area. Consult the US Plant Hardiness Zone map online at planthardiness.ars.usda.gov, or call your local Extension office for the information. Choose plants bred to be less susceptible to certain diseases because they are most likely to succeed. You will not buy all of the plants on your list. You will refine it before making your purchases.

DRAW A PLAN

It is a good idea to photograph the space where you will locate your garden. You can edit the picture digitally or print it out and draw on the image. I like to use graph paper to make a scale drawing; you may prefer an informal sketch. Whatever method you use, artistic experience is not necessary. You will need paper, a pencil, an eraser, graph paper, a ruler, and a tape measure. For your 3 by 8–foot (1 by 2.4 m) flower bed, an easy scale is 1 inch = 1 foot (2.5 cm = 0.3 m). You should note the scale on the graph paper; write the letter N and an arrow pointing north. Start your drawing with a fixed feature, such as a fence or a house corner, to indicate precisely where the garden will be. Draw your flower bed's curvy outline to scale.

Inside the garden's outline, place a focal point—remember to place it off-center for a more informal look. The focal point can be a birdbath, statue, or garden ornament such as an obelisk. Refer to your plant list and, reviewing the pictures you have marked in books and catalogs, imagine how plants will look when placed next to each other. Frame the focal point with a favorite plant shown inside a cloud shape. Write the plant's name inside the cloud; note how many you need. You may create a key if there isn't room for the plant names on the plan. Add other plants to the garden's outline. Place each variety in a group of three, five, or seven, depending on the plant's size. My clients often ask why we plant in odd numbers. It is because we want the garden to look natural, to replicate nature. Even numbers of plants are boring, especially if placed in a line; there are no rigid lines in nature. To create balance, for example, place your three plants in a triangle—giving visual variety. As a plus, your garden center may offer a discount for purchasing more than one plant. Planting your flowers in waves or groups will achieve the look of abundance you seek. When you avoid the onesie syndrome, planting many plants but with only one of each variety, your design will have cohesion.

When your plan is complete, you will have refined your list to, at most, ten plants, with one, three, five, or seven of each. Write the quantities needed next to each plant name on your list. Feel good about your list because there will be less chance of impulse buying. It's time to head to the garden center.

SELECT THE PLANTS

At the garden center, choose plants with vigorous growth. They should be well rooted but not crowded in the container. If the roots are coming through the holes in the bottom of the pot, the plant may be rootbound. Don't purchase a plant with visible signs of pests or damage. It is a plus if the plant is not blooming because it will expend energy establishing roots rather than making flowers. We want the gratification flowers give us, so selecting a plant without blooms is hard. However, resist those tempting blossoms; you will have a sturdier plant.

PREPARE THE BED

If you complete this task before you purchase your plants, you can get them into the ground sooner. My decision on when to prepare the bed usually depends upon the weather. Begin by marking the bed's borders with a water hose or spray chalk. Ensure the area is weed-free—pull any you see and remove the roots. Because we are concerned about keeping the planet clean, I do not advocate using chemicals to control weeds—you will use methods such as mulching instead. You will have had the soil tested and added any recommended amendments. As noted, organic matter dramatically improves clay and sandy soils. Add leaf mold or any organic compost, such as mushroom compost, digging 3 to 4 inches (8 to 10 cm) into the top layer of soil. Herbaceous flowers in healthy soil should not need any fertilizer.

PLANT CAREFULLY

Place your plants in their nursery containers in the positions where you will plant them, as shown in your plan, or move them around if you wish; be flexible. By measuring center to center, you will ensure enough space between each plant according to its width when fully grown. This information is on the plant label. For a cottage garden, you may plant them a little closer to achieve

The gardener collects leaves in fall and allows them to compost for use in spring at Northview.

a look of abundance, but there must be sufficient room for air circulation to avoid disease.

Make a hole twice as wide and at the same depth as the plant's pot. The soil at the top of the container should be level with the top of the hole. Carefully tilt the container and remove the plant with the other hand. Spread out the roots and place the plant in the hole, backfilling with the soil you removed. Pat the soil around the roots. Pat firmly enough to prevent air pockets but lightly enough to avoid compacting the soil.

WATER AND MULCH

Water thoroughly after planting. The new plants will need regular watering during the first year. Allow the soil to become moderately dry between waterings. Use a fingertip to check whether the soil is dry or wet. When there is no rain, water new plants deeply once a week. Always water the base area; do not shower the plant, which encourages mold and mildew. A soaker hose makes proper watering easy. Lay the soaker hose on top of the soil, near the base of plants. Attach the hose to the spigot and turn on the water at a low volume. Run the water for about thirty minutes. You do not need to move the hose. You can even hide it with mulch if you wish.

Gardeners often use bark mulch to suppress weeds and help retain water. However, because we want a look of abundance, it should be used sparingly in the cottage garden as it may inhibit the growth and spread of perennials. The best organic mulch is shredded leaves, compost, well-rotted manure, or pine needles.

The thousands of pores throughout the tubing of a soaker hose allow water to seep out at a slow, even rate.

Take a photograph of your new garden. As the season progresses, continue taking photos, especially when your flowers bloom. Next year, refer to the pictures as you plan to extend your beautiful cottage garden.

As you progress with your gardening experience, do not be discouraged by occasional disappointments or overwhelmed by environmental challenges. You will learn how to address the problems with doable solutions. The result will be a thriving garden—a source of pride and enjoyment.

Grafton Cottage garden in England has just enough lawn for the family to enjoy recreation together.

CHAPTER 2

Contemporary Challenges

When written in Chinese, the word "crisis" is composed of two characters—one represents danger and one represents opportunity.

—JOHN F. KENNEDY

Gardening has never been without its challenges. My grandmother did not complain about the obstacles she faced in her British garden, but I heard her tut-tutting when she found a snail on a plant or had difficulty removing an especially obstinate weed. These challenges persist today. In addition, we face unpredictable weather events, food insecurities, and rising prices. It is no wonder that since the onset of COVID-19 the rate of stress felt by individuals across the globe has escalated. This chapter explores these problems as they relate to the garden. Later, we will discuss how to turn each obstacle into an opportunity. You will achieve gardening success despite the challenges and do your part to mitigate the problems.

Pollution

My grandmother did not own a lawn mower. She had very little lawn—just a tiny patch of grass where my baby cousin, Marion, would lie on a blanket and coo as we worked in the garden. It was my job from a young age to keep that grass short. I would use some shears that could have been sharper; the task made the lawn seem much larger to me back then. When I finished, I basked in praise for a job well done.

Before I knew the word, I understood pollution, but it had nothing to do with the garden. Soupy smog, a mixture of fog and smoke from a nearby factory, sometimes enveloped my world and prevented me from playing outdoors. Few other pollutants were in the garden because my parents and grandparents did not use harmful chemicals. In today's world of gardening, pollution has a far-reaching impact. We can readily identify several sources of pollution and how they influence our gardening efforts.

THE PROBLEM WITH LAWNS

The problem with lawns is more than the time and effort required for their upkeep; it is also about their significant environmental impact. There are four types of pollution caused by maintaining a lawn: air pollution, water pollution, soil pollution, and noise pollution. Maintaining an area of lawn that requires fertilizing, watering, and mowing contributes to each type. In addition, light pollution has detrimental effects on plants and animals. The scale of the pollution issue is staggering.

There are 40 million acres of lawn in America. Gas-powered lawn mowers, leaf blowers, and other lawn equipment use 800 million gallons of gasoline annually. Additionally, some 17 million gallons are spilled when the equipment is filled. A lawn produces four times more carbon than it absorbs when we use gasoline, fertilizers, and pesticides to maintain it.

The time and cost of maintaining a lawn are enormous. Each homeowner spends an average of 150 hours a year tending their lawn, and Americans collectively spend $40 to $50 billion on lawn care annually. Plus, lawns need many gallons of water to thrive, more than corn or soybeans. As Doug Tallamy says in his 2020 book *Nature's Best Hope*, "We have to put the plants back" and eliminate these ecological deserts.

AIR POLLUTION

Emissions from diverse sources, including the previously mentioned lawn mower, are currently polluting our air at an alarming rate. According to the Environmental Protection Agency (EPA), an independent agency of the United States government that protects human health and the environment, six common air pollutants contribute to this urgent issue. They are carbon monoxide, fine particles, ground-level ozone, lead, nitrogen dioxide, and sulfur dioxide.

An example of an adverse effect of air pollutants is the formation of acid rain. Acid rain occurs when two common air pollutants, sulfur dioxide and nitrogen oxide, react with water, oxygen, and other chemicals to form sulfuric and nitric acids. These acid particles mix with rain, snow, fog, hail, or dust and fall to the ground. Acid rain may cause harmful effects to the soil, plants, and ponds in our gardens.

Pollutants cause environmental damage, and fine particles, such as those from wildfires, impair visibility. Breathing polluted air can directly affect our health, aggravating respiratory diseases such as asthma. The

A typical suburban American home has a large expanse of lawn area.

Stormwater runoff is not clean as it washes pollution into waterways.

unfortunate result is an increase in hospital admissions and visits to emergency rooms, affecting us and our loved ones.

WATER POLLUTION

Stormwater runoff is snow and rain that flows off the rooftops of buildings as well as parking lots, roads, and other impervious surfaces. It flows overland, or storm sewers discharge it into nearby stream beds, rivers, or lakes. According to data from the EPA, rainwater runoff accounts for 70 percent of all water pollution, a growing global crisis. Stormwater runoff is not clean; the runoff washes pollutants into waterways. Contaminants include garbage, oil and grease, gasoline, sediment from construction sites, road salt, lawn pesticides, agricultural herbicides, heavy metals from roof shingles, pet waste, and illicit discharges such as paints, cleaning solution products, and used motor oil. Stormwater contaminated with pollutants harms fish and wildlife, kills native vegetation, and fouls drinking water supplies.

SOIL POLLUTION

Soil is polluted when it contains toxic chemicals in high enough concentrations to pose a risk to human health and the ecosystem. The Soil Science Society of America defines a soil pollutant as any substance in the soil that exceeds naturally occurring levels and poses human health risks. One way soil becomes polluted is with insecticides, herbicides, and fertilizers used by gardeners and farmers. Rachel Carson's 1962 book *Silent Spring* spurred pesticide regulation in the United States and the formation of the EPA. Unfortunately, according to the Brookings Institution, a nonprofit organization conducting nonpartisan research in Washington, DC, the United States must catch up with other countries in regulating herbicides, pesticides, and fertilizers. From personal experience, I notice synthetic pesticides disappearing from garden centers in England. Synthetic pesticides are compounds produced by people through an industrial process. The Royal Horticultural Society stopped selling all pesticides in early 2023. In the United States, however, many are commercially available to gardeners at retail garden stores.

At my home, Astolat Farm, we are searching for a farmer who farms organically, but we have yet to be successful. Our current farmer does not use organic products as he farms as his father and ancestors farmed before him. He uses the same methods as all farmers in this agricultural area. We are grateful that he works our land because, if not farmed, the aggressive, invasive trees and shrubs such as multiflora rose (*Rosa multiflora*), Russian olive (*Elaeagnus angustifolia*), and barberry (*Berberis thunbergii*) would become dominant. However, we persist in our search for a more environmentally friendly option.

The lower field at Astolat Farm and its proximity to the kitchen garden causes concern because of today's farming methods.

NOISE POLLUTION

Consider the personal implications of noise pollution. The World Health Organization estimates that one in three people in Europe is affected by traffic noise. In the United States, tens of millions of Americans suffer from a range of health issues, including heart disease and hearing loss, due to noise exposure. It's important to note that mowers, leaf blowers, and other power gardening equipment are the leading causes of noise pollution in our gardens, directly impacting our daily lives.

LIGHT POLLUTION

An article in *National Geographic* magazine opened my eyes, so to speak, to the problem of light pollution. Light pollution is the artificial lighting of the night sky by cars, streetlamps, offices, factories, outdoor advertising, and buildings. I would add ornamental lighting found in many suburban and rural flower gardens. Outdoor artificial light affects human health, wildlife behavior, and our ability to observe stars and other celestial objects.

I planted native shrubs in the cottage garden, including this Diervilla lonicera, *commonly referred to as northern bush honeysuckle, and the ninebark (*Physocarpus*) next to it.*

Phlox in my cutting garden is one of many native plants.

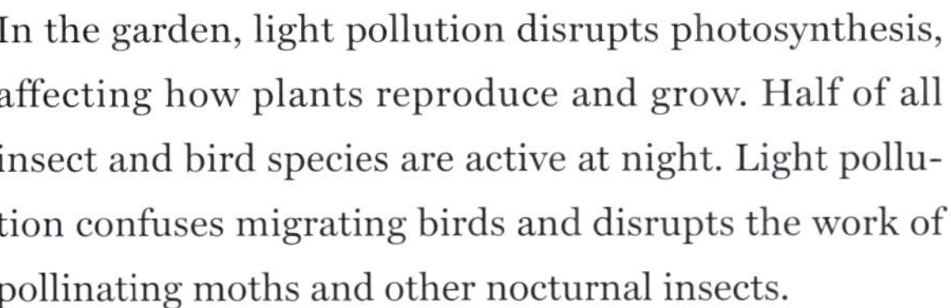

In the garden, light pollution disrupts photosynthesis, affecting how plants reproduce and grow. Half of all insect and bird species are active at night. Light pollution confuses migrating birds and disrupts the work of pollinating moths and other nocturnal insects.

WHAT CAN WE DO?

Fortunately, the power to make a difference lies in the hands of home gardeners. By adopting sustainable gardening practices, such as planting native species, embracing the beauty of natural imperfections, using organic insect repellents and encouraging natural predators, and reducing the size of lawns, we can begin to reverse the damage. In upcoming chapters, I share my journey practicing sustainable gardening and managing pollution issues in my cottage garden. I invite you to join me in this endeavor. Together, our collective efforts can lead to the restoration of healthy ecosystems.

*Snowdrops (*Galanthus*) and other spring blooms appear two or more weeks earlier than in previous years.*

Extreme Weather

The timing of plant development throughout the year has changed in my garden, and I see some spring-blooming plants flowering in December. I can grow flowers that, previously, I would see thriving only in more southern climates. Unpredictable weather events are escalating here. I have experienced rainstorms dumping up to 4 inches (10 cm) of rain in a short period, high winds downing trees, a winter with very little snow, and heat waves lasting several weeks as early as June. I am more fortunate than people in other areas of the country who have suffered through tornadoes, very high winds, extreme flooding, rampant wildfires, and severe drought.

THE SCIENCE BEHIND EXTREME WEATHER

According to NASA's Goddard Institute for Space Studies, the vast majority (97 percent) of climate scientists agree we are in the midst of global warming, with the earth's rapid warming in the last two decades. The leading science organizations worldwide have issued publications expressing the conclusion that humans are responsible for this phenomenon due to burning fossil fuels. It is important to remember that scientists focus on evidence, not opinions.

The reality of global warming is alarming. It directly results from releasing heat-trapping gases, known as greenhouse gases, such as carbon monoxide, methane, and nitrous oxide. These emissions are causing extreme weather, melting glaciers, and warming oceans. The

Snowfalls like this one, seen through my bedroom window, are becoming rare.

main contributors to this crisis are fossil fuels—coal, gas, and oil. A National Oceanic and Atmospheric Administration study reveals that greenhouse gas levels are increasing yearly. Global greenhouse gas levels rose to 50 percent more than before the Industrial Revolution. This means there were about 50 percent more carbon dioxide molecules in the air than in about 1750, trapping heat and warming the planet. Scientists have set a climate goal of limiting global warming to 1.5°C (34.7°F), but this target is becoming increasingly difficult to reach. A United Nations panel has issued a stark warning that humanity is running out of time to avert some of the worst effects of this crisis.

WILDFIRES

An increase in the number, severity, and duration of wildfires is another indicator of how the world is becoming warmer. The EPA reports that, since 1983, the National Interagency Fire Center has documented an average of about 70,000 wildfires per year. The extent to which areas are burning is increasing. Moreover, the peak of the US wildfire season appears to be earlier. Wildfires burn forests, shrublands, and grasslands, which are essential ecosystems, both environmentally and economically. Furthermore, even in communities far downwind, wildfire smoke causes poor air quality that can lead to significant health problems.

IMPACT ON ANIMALS

Rapid environmental changes directly and indirectly affect animals worldwide. The warming climate affects the ecosystem and food chain to which an animal has adapted. As a result, some species are migrating in search of new places to live. The Nature Conservancy uses science to identify suitable locations and works with local partners and communities to do everything it can to protect these environments.

IMPACT ON AGRICULTURE

Global warming presents real threats to agricultural production. In the United States, heavy precipitation can harm crops by eroding soil and depleting soil nutrients. Heavy rains can also increase agricultural runoff into oceans, lakes, and streams. This runoff can harm water quality. On its website, the United States Department of Agriculture (USDA) identifies five climate vulnerabilities:

1. Decreased agricultural productivity
2. Threat to water quality and quantity
3. Disproportionate impacts on vulnerable communities
4. Shocks due to extreme climate events
5. Stress on infrastructure and public lands

The USDA outlines an action plan for dealing with the problems and providing hope. In addition, the United Nations argues that the world is progressing with cheaper solar and wind power and better accessibility to electric vehicles. Governments and businesses are investing large sums in clean energy.

Wheat is one crop grown at Astolat Farm. Heavy rains are frequent now and harm crop production.

Experts agree that individuals can make a difference. I want to be one of those individuals. Let me show you in forthcoming chapters how I adapted my cottage garden to the effects of extreme weather.

Food Supply Shortages and High Prices

The COVID-19 pandemic disrupted our way of life and changed it forever. Like many, I began to order groceries online for my husband to pick up or for the store to deliver. The rise in e-commerce continued after the pandemic as online shopping increased exponentially, not only for food but also for many other services—even doctor's appointments are now frequently held virtually.

You may choose to grow vegetables in your front yard during difficult times.

Throughout the pandemic we experienced many shortages because of supply chain delays. With the lack of fresh vegetables, many grew their food for the first time.

FOOD AVAILABILITY

According to a US Chamber of Commerce report, there were no supply shortages by 2024 as the pandemic was over. However, environmental challenges and labor shortages caused temporary problems with the availability of certain items. Avian flu spreading to the dairy industry threatened to disrupt the supply of dairy products and eggs. Extreme weather events in India and Vietnam jeopardized the supply of spices and sugar exports. A warming planet and water pollution continue to negatively impact fish populations. The quality, variety, and quantity of fresh produce available in stores also decreased. The home gardening trend continues as a result.

RISING FOOD PRICES

Although the food supply may have been less disrupted by 2024, the cost of food soared. According to the Consumer Price Index, in the four years between 2020 and 2024, grocery prices jumped by 25 percent in the United States, outpacing overall inflation of 19 percent during the same period. As a result, food insecurity rose, and food banks around the country continued to report significant increases in demand. About 49 million people in the United States rely on charities like Feeding America. Food insecurity is found in every corner of the United States, having particular impact on children, senior citizens, people of color, and those living below the poverty threshold.

Let us be honest—the contemporary challenges the world is facing are daunting. It is easy to feel overwhelmed by how big the problems are. It is impossible to save the whole world, but I can start where I am. I have found so many answers in my beautiful cottage garden. For example, I can grow an extra row of vegetables and donate them to my local food pantry. I will share this and other ways to help as we journey together.

Grow an extra row of vegetables and donate them to a food pantry.

During the COVID-19 crisis, I designed and created my new meadow garden.

Stressful Living and the Changing Workplace

I fared better than many through the COVID-19 crisis because I spent those days of social isolation working outdoors in the garden or indoors making plans for the garden. I never felt lonely because my mind was busy with gardening plans and ideas—so the lockdown didn't bother me too much. Surrounded by beauty and peace, I designed and created new gardens, including a meadow garden, and improved established ones. For many other people, it was a different story. "In the first year of the COVID-19 pandemic, the global prevalence of anxiety and depression increased by a massive 25 percent," the World Health Organization (WHO) stated in a 2024 scientific brief. Surveys by the Pew Research Center revealed that four in ten US adults (41 percent) experienced high levels of psychological distress.

During the pandemic, many people worked from home. This trend continues today. Another study by the Pew Research Center (2024) shows around 22 million, roughly 14 percent of employed adults in the United States, work from home all the time, while 41 percent of remote workers work part-time on a hybrid schedule. Many workers and employers prefer this arrangement. However, a *USA Today* survey of 667 remote workers shows the downside of working from home, with 34 percent feeling isolated. Other challenges from working at

My garden provides healing and solace in troubling times.

home were cited: feeling more depressed (11 percent) and feeling more stressed or burnt out (9 percent).

I'm sorry to say I feel more discouraged post-COVID-19, but not because of feelings of social isolation as I work from home. I am very disheartened about world events. Today's distressing news items include international conflict, natural disasters, and political unrest. Incredibly upsetting are the wars in the Middle East and a politically divided nation at home. I want information but need to limit my news and social media time. I must focus on things I can control. I focus on my garden. It is well documented that gardening is an antidote to stress. A garden provides the healing and solace needed in troubling times. I will show you how.

Looking to the Future

In this book's first part, we looked at a traditional English cottage garden, its history, and how to create one. I then outline some of today's global challenges. In the second part, I suggest ways to meet those challenges, beginning with how we can prevent pollution by gardening sustainably. I give you some powerful tools for contributing to a healthier planet, creating a flourishing garden, and becoming a stress-free gardener. The section concludes with an optimistic view of the future as you'll learn how to involve children and leave a legacy.

PART II

CONFRONTING THE CHALLENGES

It is time to stop the debate over climate change and take action. Replace the wastelands we call lawns with meadows.

CHAPTER 3

Prevent Pollution

What you do makes a difference, and you have to decide what kind of difference you want to make.

—DR. JANE GOODALL

My father and maternal grandfather were coal miners in the West Midlands of England, known as the Black Country, a name that symbolized the pervasive smoke that shrouded the towns and cities in the area. Despite this, my family was fortunate to live near a hundred square miles of forest called Cannock Chase, a haven of natural beauty. The Chase, as we affectionately called it, was my playground, a place where the air was noticeably cleaner, a stark contrast to the coal-filled atmosphere just a few miles away.

My father began work in a coal mine when he was fourteen years old, digging underground for fifty years. He was proud of his hard work in the mines. He would tell me that the power of coal had built our civilization for 200 years. Indeed, the standard of living improved enormously in my father's lifetime. He was unaware that fossil fuels were causing the rise of carbon dioxide and methane levels in the atmosphere, leading to a rapidly overheating planet.

The United States is polarized about humans' role in global warming. One side of the debate believes it is man-made, while the other side maintains it is due to natural causes. Gardeners agree, however, that highly variable weather events ARE occurring, whatever the cause. They know ecosystem productivity is altering; for example, there is a spread of invasive species and less biodiversity. Gardeners understand pollution is not good for our gardens. Therefore, whichever theory you support, it is time to stop the debate and move on to do all we can to protect our precious, fragile natural world. We need strategies to deal with the changes we see in our gardens. We can start by gardening as sustainably as possible so our valued wildlife is preserved. I will show you some sustainable methods I use in my cottage garden. I will explain how to build a meadow as an alternative to the wastelands we call lawns.

Sustainable Cottage Gardening

A first step toward taking a stand against pollution is to garden in a way that does not harm our planet and its inhabitants. To this end, I use sustainable methods that add to the earth rather than take away from it. These practices include using compost, applying fewer chemicals, conserving water, removing invasive plant species, and growing native plants. If you follow some of the earth-friendly gardening procedures I describe, you will reap (pardon the pun) numerous benefits.

MAKE AND USE COMPOST

Compost is frequently called black gold because of its value in improving garden soil. Penn State Extension describes compost as "organic matter that has decomposed into a form that plants can use." Composting occurs daily in soil, but when you create a compost pile, you speed up the natural processes. Bacteria, fungi, and other microbes feed on organic matter in the first stage; centipedes, millipedes, sowbugs, and other organisms continue the decomposition. The body heat of the microorganisms causes the temperature in the pile to rise—it should reach a temperature of 110°F to 140°F (43.3°C to 60°C) in four to five days. The heating kills some weed seeds and disease organisms in the center but not toward the cooler outside; therefore, turn the pile regularly to heat all parts. Turning adds oxygen to the center of the pile, speeding up decomposition.

Compost is simple to make from organic materials such as plants, weeds, prunings, lawn clippings, leaves, vegetable and fruit scraps, and paper items. A good mix consists of two parts browns—for example, dead leaves—and one part greens, such as fresh grass clippings. Do not compost diseased plants, plants that have gone to seed, meat and dairy products, vegetables cooked with animal fats, or human or pet feces. The process can be as simple as making a heap of yard and kitchen waste and allowing it to decay, or by using a compost bin. My grandfather merely did the former. When I was small, my grandmother would hand me a bowl of potato peelings to carry to Grandpa's compost pile. I would tip them on top of the pile and run indoors out of the English rain, only needing to return to retrieve the potato peeler I inadvertently threw out with the peelings.

There is no need to rake up and remove every leaf from your lawn in the autumn. Doug Tallamy, a professor at the University of Delaware, stresses the ecological value of leaf litter. Tallamy says leaf litter should be called leaf largess. Run a lawn mower over fallen leaves a couple of times and place the shredded leaves inside a circle of chicken wire or into a wooden bin. I use the resulting leaf mold to compost or top-dress my flower beds. Mulching with shredded leaves is particularly useful when delicate plants have difficulty pushing through

We must preserve valuable wildlife, such as the beautiful bluebirds at my meadow's edge.

Compost is frequently called black gold.

Place shredded leaves in a container and leave them to become excellent leaf mold.

I have three compost bins. The one on the left is a rotating barrel that allows the compost materials to be turned easily.

heavier products. Leaf mold is one of my favorite soil amendments.

You can make a compost bin by wiring old wooden pallets together or you may purchase a plastic bin with holes in the sides to allow air transfer. The microbes in the compost need water and oxygen, so it is essential to keep your pile as damp as a wrung-out sponge and to break up large pieces, turning it frequently to ensure air reaches the center. One of my current compost bins is a rotating barrel that facilitates turning.

Place your heap or bin on a level spot near the garden and a water source, in sun or shade. Your compost is ready for use when it looks dark and crumbly and none of the starting materials are visible. Use your black gold as a mulch or top-dressing to amend the soil before planting, or as a potting soil additive. In this way, you are using natural amendments rather than purchasing them or using something chemical.

Following the advice of New England gardener and author Sydney Eddison, I put a layer of compost on my flower and vegetable garden beds every year in early spring to improve the structure and health of the soil. I don't have enough homemade compost for this large task so I purchase a load of mushroom compost from my local supplier.

I recently discovered the soil improvement benefits of a black, lightweight, fine-grained substance called biochar, a carbon-rich substance made from burning organic material from agricultural and forestry wastes called biomass. The process reduces the level of carbon dioxide in the atmosphere. Biochar is an organic material that can last for thousands of years in the ground. I added some to the soil at the base of a rhododendron shrub where there is considerable soil degradation from an adjacent road. I see improvement in my rhododendron, although it is still in the early stages.

When purchasing biochar, however, I check that it is made from wood harvested from forests in the United States and certified for use in organic gardens and farms, because some manufacturers use treated sewage sludge to make the product with a process called pyrolysis. A review of 259 studies by Mendel University in Brno, Czech Republic, raised concerns about the long-term safety of its use. A review of similar studies in the *International Journal of Environmental Research and Public Health* led the authors to suggest not using biochar on edible plants to mitigate these concerns.

NO-DIG GARDENING

Compost has an active role in the no-dig gardening method, sometimes called lasagna gardening. I adopted the no-dig approach when I made my first garden at Astolat Farm. Our acreage was a clean slate for locating my new flower beds at that time. But I knew exactly where I wanted to start. As I mentioned, I wanted a beautiful view from my favorite chair in the Garden Room. I designed the garden I would name Serenity, a healing garden. I outlined a curvy bed with rocks and took my garden spade to start digging. I was younger and more robust then, but I still couldn't get my spade to penetrate the hard ground. Pocono soil is clay and rocks; it seems to grow rocks. I now understood the local joke, "What do you call a trowel in the Poconos?" The answer, "A backhoe!"

Not owning a backhoe, I remembered my grandfather's advice. When I was a child, he told me, "Use all that black gold to make a bed on top of the ground." No digging required. This method, often called lasagna

Gather the materials for your new lasagna garden.

Mark the edge of the new garden. I used rocks.

Wetting every layer of the lasagna garden is vital.

gardening, is one I've adapted for many of my flower beds. The procedure is as follows:

1. Gather the materials. You will need newspaper, compost, composted cow manure, and good topsoil. Composted cow manure is safe for plants. Newspaper is biodegradable. The newspaper industry uses soy ink for the majority of newspaper print these days, even for colored pictures. However, it is not a good idea to use glossy paper that may contain toxins. Using any newspaper is a personal preference. As an organic gardener, I don't use it where I grow vegetables because the soy farmer may have used GMOs.
2. If the area is grass-covered, mow it short before you begin. Mine was bare soil as I repurposed an area where I removed some invasive grasses. Mark the new bed with paint or use a garden hose. I put rocks around the new garden's edging. Next to it, I made a small stone patio where I could sit and enjoy the flowers.
3. Wet the area thoroughly.
4. Cover the bed with newspaper, two layers thick, and water again until the paper is thoroughly wet. If the weather is windy, use some rocks to hold the newspaper down before spraying. When it is wet, the newspaper will stay in place.
5. Add about 4 inches (10 cm) of compost. If it is a large bed and I don't have enough homemade compost, I use mushroom compost that the local landscape supply store delivers.
6. Wet the compost, add another two layers of newspaper, and wet it again.

7. Mix composted cow manure with homemade or mushroom compost. Spread a 3-inch (7.6 cm) layer on the new bed. Always use composted animal manures as raw manure will scorch the plants' roots. Next, you've guessed it, wet thoroughly.
8. Purchase an excellent topsoil for the final layer that should be about 6 inches (15.2 cm) deep.
9. Wet the finished area well and let it settle for two or three weeks before planting. Your finished bed will be 14 to 15 inches (35 to 38 cm) high before settling a few inches lower.

I planted all white flowers in the new bed. White plants are an appropriate addition to my Serenity Garden. An added advantage is that a white garden, often called a moon garden, can be enjoyed after dark.

When I came to America, I learned that many methods of lasagna gardening are practiced in this country. While there is no right or wrong way, I no longer use my grandfather's favorite peat moss as a layer; I use composted cow manure instead. Peat moss is banned in England nowadays, but it is still available in America, where it is acquired mainly from Canada. It has excellent benefits in the garden, but its harvesting is environmentally unsound. Peat moss is found in the Northern Hemisphere in marshy bogs that cover 2 percent of earth's land. The bogs store one-third of the world's soil carbon. When you harvest peat moss, you release harmful carbon dioxide into the environment.

Peat moss grows very slowly, and we are harvesting it faster than it can be produced so it is essentially nonrenewable. Some sustainable alternatives are coconut coir, pine needles, rice hulls, composted manure, leaf mold, and regular compost. Coir is the fibrous material

Rake about 4 inches (10 cm) of compost over the newspaper.

Mix composted cow manure with mushroom compost and spread it on the bed.

Spread a good-quality topsoil for the final layer.

Let the finished bed settle for two or three weeks, then plant your beautiful lasagna garden.

The white garden's first year.

The grass areas at Astolat Farm are less than perfect. We mow the weeds.

between the shell and the outer coating of the coconut. It has no nutrients but has excellent drainage qualities. I use coir instead of peat moss in raised beds and for starting plants from seeds indoors and in the greenhouse.

When purchasing plants, be aware they are often potted in a peat mix. For this reason, I look for bare-root perennials when possible. Bare-root plants are field-grown and sold with no soil or compost. I usually purchase mine online. I receive them while the plant is dormant, between October and March. They are easy to plant; follow the nursery's instructions and keep them well watered.

USE FEWER CHEMICAL FERTILIZERS, PESTICIDES, AND HERBICIDES

An easy way to lessen the use of chemicals and prevent pollution is to reduce the size of your lawn. You don't need to remove all of it; a small lawn surrounded by a border of cottage garden plants looks lovely. The remaining turfgrass can be something other than golf course perfect. I don't use chemicals on my lawn; we mow the weeds and throw clover seeds on the bare spots. Visitors to my gardens focus on the flowers, never the grass.

A valuable hint related to lawn mowing is to stop raking grass clippings. Returning them to the soil keeps the carbon out of the atmosphere and creates valuable organic matter.

Britain and some areas of America have adopted a No Mow May initiative. However, homeowners may balk at the untidy effect and possibly the spread of dandelions and other weeds. Benjamin Vogt, author of *Prairie Up: An Introduction to Natural Garden Design*, says not mowing for a month will encourage the growth of weeds and aggressive and invasive plants. A more beautiful option is to consider planting a meadow.

Do not remove spent flowers at season's end—pollinators need them.

Handpick Japanese beetles and drop them into a jar of soapy water.

Adding a layer of compost to the flower and vegetable gardens in spring reduces the need for chemical fertilizers. If I need to fertilize, an organic one such as fish emulsion provides the required nutrients in my garden. Be guided by the results of your soil test.

I use an integrated pest management approach (IPM) that begins with the following eleven nonchemical control strategies for pests and diseases:

1. Learn to tolerate some damage. This is not easy if, like me, you want your garden to look perfect, but most plants can endure 20 to 30 percent leaf defoliation. At the end of the season, don't be in a hurry to remove untidy, spent flowers because they may still attract pollinators.
2. Wait for the predators to arrive. Don't be alarmed by aphids feeding in spring; ladybugs and other natural predators usually clean up the infestation in a month or so.
3. Spray with water. Try spraying with a strong water stream to dislodge aphids and mites.
4. Remove and dispose of badly damaged plants. Removal may minimize the problem spreading to adjacent plants and prevent recurrence.
5. Handpick. Pick off insects such as Japanese beetles that are very destructive to plants. Drop them into a jar of soapy water. They will suffocate and die quickly. This is considered a humane

Floating row covers are an effective barrier against pests.

way of dealing with these pests. Do this for egg masses, also.

6. Choose pest-resistant plants. Check the label on new plant purchases for resistance or tolerance to pests and diseases.
7. Rotate crops. Move your vegetables around your garden beds, planting them in different spots each year.
8. Use barriers. Exclude pests with floating row covers, paper collars (for cutworms), and diatomaceous earth (for slugs). Diatomaceous earth is a powder made from naturally occurring sedimentary rock. It has an abrasive feel that slugs avoid crossing.
9. Do not overfertilize. Aphids and spider mites create more offspring on overfertilized plants.
10. Hand-pull weeds. Hand-pull or hoe weeds while they are seedlings.
11. Monitor your plants. Check your plants weekly for problems, flipping over leaves and examining the undersides. Regular monitoring lets you catch most problems before they get out of hand.

To sum up, IPM means managing problems by using physical and cultural methods first and applying a least-toxic pesticide as a last resort. My pesticide of choice is horticultural soap.

SAVE WATER

Conserving water becomes increasingly important with the unpredictable weather events we are experiencing. Several ways to save water include reducing lawn areas, adding rain barrels, and using mulches.

Collecting water in rain barrels, if allowed by your state and local laws, is a wise practice for water conservation. Place a rain barrel under a downspout to collect water from the roof when it rains; save the collected rainwater for the plants in your yard during the hot summer months. Since rain barrels reduce the water that runs off your property, fewer pollutants (such as motor oil residue, road salt, fertilizers, and pesticides from lawns) enter local streams and rivers. As an added benefit, rainwater contains nitrogen in the form of nitrate caused by lightning and electrification in the atmosphere. Unlike some tap water, it does not have chlorine or fluoride. Plants need nitrogen; chlorine and fluoride are detrimental to them.

Some gardeners collect gray water from showers, sinks, and washing machines. Gray water is lightly used household wastewater that contains no toilet waste. The practice is acceptable if you use plant-friendly products to wash dishes and clothes. I know of a gardener who places an empty bucket in the shower stall before turning on the faucet. The bucket collects the water while it is reaching the temperature she requires. I sometimes reuse the water in which I have steamed vegetables, as long as I have not added salt.

Be sure to water your plants correctly. First, check that watering is necessary by testing the soil with your finger. Poke your finger close to the plant's stem to feel the soil near the root zone. If the soil feels dry, direct the water to the base of the plant using a watering can or a watering wand attached to a hose to avoid wetting the leaves, which can cause powdery mildew and other diseases. It is best to water slowly and deeply only those plants that need it. I call this precision watering. I prefer to water with a watering can.

Rain barrels lessen the water that runs off your property, reducing stream pollutants.

With a watering can, I can better control where the water goes, knowing I should water at the roots, not showering indiscriminately with a hose. Also, I can easily control which plants need water that day. My husband and I have developed a system to make watering my garden manageable. At the end of the day, when he goes outside to feed the goats, my husband fills numerous watering cans from rain barrels. He places the filled cans around the gardens where he knows I need them. The following day, when I make my daily tour, I can complete the watering task more quickly.

Inexpensive watering cans are my preferred choice for watering plants.

My husband places watering cans filled with rainwater where I need them.

You may purchase a drip irrigation system with a timer for the vegetable garden.

Besides watering cans and watering wands, two other watering methods are a drip system and a soaker hose. Both direct the water to the roots. Drip irrigation is a system of tubes and nozzles (emitters) that the gardener installs so each emitter releases water slowly at the plant's base. You can attach a simple battery-powered timer when you are not home. Drip systems are appropriate for vegetable gardens that need regular watering throughout the season. They require frequent checking and repair as needed. They can be 90 percent efficient when correctly installed and maintained.

Soaker hoses are great for new garden beds that you must water frequently until the plants are established. Soaker hoses are plastic, rubber, or canvas hoses with tiny holes. They are much cheaper than drip irrigation systems. Some permeate water through their entire surface. I wind one around the plants in a new bed, attach the garden hose, and turn the spigot slightly, letting the water run for ten to twenty minutes. I turn it off manually, but you could use a timer-controlled valve. I check my soaker hoses at the beginning of each year for sun damage and uniform water distribution. They can cut water use by as much as 70 percent.

A 2- to 3-inch (5 to 7.6 cm) layer of mulch helps the soil retain water while suppressing weeds and protecting against temperature extremes. In addition, mulch reduces soil erosion and crusting while increasing water penetration into the soil. Mulch also enhances your garden's appearance. Gardeners cultivate mulched soil less frequently; we now know less soil disturbance is best. Tilling the soil destroys beneficial microorganisms like bacteria and fungi, leads to compaction and poor drainage so plant roots can't penetrate, increases erosion, and brings weed seeds to the surface. I mulch with shredded leaves, pine needles, finely shredded cedar mulch, or gravel. Several bark mulches are available; I use cedar because it contains a chemical that repels fungi, such as the destructive artillery fungus that shoots spores onto your house or car.

I prefer cedar mulch to any other wood bark mulch.

Types of Mulch

Straw is a suitable mulch for the vegetable garden. Apply mulch for winter protection in late fall, once the soil has cooled but before it has frozen. Then reapply in mid-spring once the soil has warmed. Low-growing plants, often called groundcovers, such as sedums, make excellent mulches.

One of my favorite mulches is shredded leaves.

Gravel also makes a great mulch.

Low-Growing Plants to Use As Mulch

*Lamium and creeping Jenny (*Lysimachia nummularia*) are fast-spreading options.*

*My favorite groundcover, less aggressive than lamium, is the beautiful blue plumbago (*Ceratostigma plumbaginoides*).*

Low-growing sedums are beautiful groundcovers.

REMOVE INVASIVE SPECIES

When I first came to Astolat Farm thirty-plus years ago, I was enchanted with the pretty white and pale pink flowers that filled the old orchard with blooms and delicate scent in late spring. Duane called them sticker bushes, and I soon learned the thorns of these shrubs give a nasty bite. The shrub is, of course, multiflora rose, a very invasive plant. When Duane decided to clean out the overgrown orchard and make it into our Woodland Walk, he had a mammoth task ahead. The multiflora rose is not the only invasive plant in there: Autumn olive (*Elaeagnus umbellata*), Japanese barberry, and bush honeysuckle (*Lonicera maackii*) also abound. He pulled them out and cut them back—to say it was hard work is an understatement. It was impossible to eliminate all of them, but they were now somewhat under control.

Japanese stiltgrass (*Microstegium vimineum*) is a more recent invasive plant species that abounds where I live. Privet (*Ligustrum*), burning bush (*Euonymus alatus*), and Japanese knotweed (*Reynoutria japonica*) are other invasive plants to avoid. Invasive plants compete with and outgrow surrounding plants. Invasive species can upset the delicate balance of a local ecosystem and even make some native plants extinct. Therefore, it is essential to remove invasive species and restore native plant communities. Japanese stiltgrass is found across most of the eastern United States and as far west as Texas. It is difficult to remove. An annual, it dies at the end of the growing season but spreads seeds liberally. The seeds can live in the ground for years. It is crucial to cut it down before it sets seed. I have had some success smothering the area with cardboard that I leave in place until it disintegrates.

Gooseneck loosestrife has interesting flowers but spreads aggressively.

The leaves of gooseneck loosestrife have a lovely fall color.

I planted Zebra grass next to the pond to provide shade for the fish. It grew aggressively by the weeping Norway spruce and was difficult to eradicate.

One of the worst invasive plants is purple loosestrife (*Lythrum salicaria*), so invasive that its rampant growth threatens wildlife and wetlands throughout the country. It chokes out native plants that are integral parts of the natural ecosystem.

Invasive and aggressive plants are not the same. Aggressive plants, like mint and dandelions, are fast-growing and -spreading, but they cannot compete with and outgrow surrounding plants like invasives. I grow gooseneck loosestrife (*Lysimachia clethroides*), which spreads aggressively by underground roots. I love it enough to spend time pulling it out of areas where I don't want it to spread. The flowers are attractive and the fall colors of the leaves are beautiful. However, I recommend it for your garden only if you want to spend time keeping it under control.

Gooseneck loosestrife and *Vinca minor*, which my mother-in-law called periwinkle, are on the invasive plants watch list in Pennsylvania. My mother-in-law loved vinca's tiny blue flowers and planted them on the property long before I moved there. It has since spread into the Woodland Walk and is very difficult to eradicate. I do not recommend this plant.

Zebra grass (*Miscanthus sinensis*) is also on Pennsylvania's watch list. Many years ago, before I trained as a master gardener, I planted one next to the pond to shade the fish. The nearby weeping Norway spruce (*Picea abies* 'Pendula') was not big enough to create shade at that time. What a mistake it was. The miscanthus grew 12 to 15 feet (3.6 to 4.6 m), swamping the weeping spruce. You can see it in many pictures in this book.

Vinca has spread aggressively at Astolat Farm.

A rock pedestal holds a pot of spring flowers where the former miscanthus grew.

Eradication was a problem as miscanthus spreads by abundant rhizomes that are impossible to dig out. The only recommended method is to use an herbicide, which is not an option in my world of sustainable gardening, especially next to a fishpond. I decided to try smothering, a process where you cut the plant down low at the end of the season and cover it with thick layers of cardboard. This deprives the plant of light and eventually kills it. In spring, there were still a couple of leaves pushing up. I added more cardboard, and a friend built a rock base to hold a slab of Pennsylvania bluestone. I now have a beautiful stand for a potted plant, and the weeping spruce is no longer hidden by an invasive tall grass. I imagine the miscanthus roots are attempting to escape underneath the plant's rocky prison, but my method is working so far.

As gardeners, you play a crucial role in environmental conservation. It's important to research which plants pose a problem in your region and avoid buying and growing them. The US Arboretum website provides very useful information. If you have any questions, don't hesitate to speak with experts at nature preserves, botanical gardens, and local Extension services.

Deer, one of our most destructive wildlife, do not eat invasive plants. It is vital to control the deer population. I've (almost) successfully stopped deer and rabbits from consuming my plants by spraying a deterrent that makes flowers and foliage less palatable. There are several brands to choose from, and they do not harm the animals. I start the season with one and change the brand when the animals become accustomed to it. It is essential to spray often.

My husband will trap groundhogs, another problem, and relocate them. Invasive Asian jumping worms (*Amynthas agrestis*) can be found in more than thirty states in the United States. While native earthworms benefit soil health, Asian jumping worms voraciously consume rich organic material and deposit hard, grainy

*The entry garden at Astolat Farm contains native plants: blazing star (*Liatris kobold*), purple coneflower, and garden phlox (*Phlox paniculata *'David').*

pellets that do not break down. The result is soil of poor structure and nutrition. Bigger than earthworms, these invasives are incredibly active, jumping and thrashing about when disturbed. You can identify them by the light-colored band called a clitellum. The band is flat and completely encircles the body. The native earthworm has a raised clitellum that only partially surrounds the body. The jumping worm spreads through its eggs that survive the winter. They are displacing valuable earthworms. The eggs are found in mulch, potted plants, and potting mixes. It is crucial to inspect these purchases carefully. (Another good reason to buy bare-root plants.) If you find one of these pests, seal it in a plastic bag and place it in the sun for a few hours. Dispose of the bag in the trash.

RESTORE NATIVE PLANT COMMUNITIES

The Pennsylvania Department of Conservation and Natural Resources describes a native plant as one that occurred within a region before settlement by Europeans. In Pennsylvania, for example, native plants include the ferns, grasses, perennial and annual wildflowers, woody trees, shrubs, and vines that covered Penn's Woods when the first settlers arrived.

There are compelling reasons to plant natives in your garden. Native plants preserve the area's biodiversity, meaning the number and variety of living things in a specific region. Our native wildlife, especially birds, butterflies, pollinators, and other organisms, evolved with the plants native to the area; many can feed only on plants they co-evolved with. If your garden has no native plants, it becomes an ecological desert for the pollinating insects essential to our survival. Without insects to pollinate our crops, we would have none to harvest. Humans would need to perform the task, as in China where they use costly hand pollination for some fruit crops due to the lack of pollinating bees. Additionally, native plants are needed to support songbirds by supplying food for the insects most baby birds require. They provide the habitat (food, cover, and places to rear their young) that wildlife needs. Without native plants, our wildlife is at risk of extinction.

Native plants are not invasive. A non-native plant is one growing outside its natural range. Some non-native plants have become invasive, aggressively spreading into natural areas and threatening our native plant communities. Some native plants are more aggressive than others, but that does not make them invasive. Using regionally appropriate, site-appropriate native plants reduces the risk of introducing an invasive exotic. Native plants provide year-round beauty. From flowers in spring and summer to brilliant fall colors and interesting bark in winter, native plants give four seasons of loveliness. You can find a native alternative with similar color, texture, or habit as a substitute for most exotic plants. It is easy to have a beautiful garden and help the ecosystem simultaneously.

You may have a fondness for a particular plant or feel strongly that a certain plant would enhance your garden's appearance. Despite it being non-native, by all means include it in your landscape as long as it is not invasive. I did not plant my garden with 100 percent natives because I wanted some plants that were traditional to the cottage garden style, although they are not native to my area. Every plant is built of carbon and deposits some into the ground through its roots, improving the carbon imbalance. However, most of the plants I grow are native.

Do not take native plants from the wild because this threatens their populations and disrupts the ecosystem. Purchase from a reputable source. Your favorite nursery may stock them, or you may wish to visit one specializing in natives.

Here are some suggestions for using native plants:

- Integrate them into your perennial borders. A blending of natives and non-natives is suitable for many sites.
- Naturalize a large area, such as a meadow or woodland, with more aggressive natives such as sunflowers (*Heliopsis helianthoides*), asters (*Symphyotrichum novae-angliae*), and black-eyed Susans (*Rudbeckia hirta*).
- Replace unsightly and invasive plants with natives.
- Reduce the size of your lawn by adding a bed of native plants.
- Create a butterfly garden, like the entry garden at Astolat Farm.
- Make a rain garden filled with native plants that like wet conditions.

One of my favorite native plants is twinleaf (*Jeffersonia diphylla*), an ephemeral that appears in spring and disappears after it has made its seeds. I grow it with other ephemerals in the Woodland Walk. I love it for its seed pods that look like Kermit the Frog; they always make me smile.

Remember to include native shrubs. Three favorites in my cottage garden are dwarf ninebark (*Physocarpus*

*Swamp milkweed (*Asclepias incarnata*) growing in my rain garden is the host plant for monarch butterflies.*

Butterfly weed is also a monarch host.

Plant a meadow with more aggressive natives such as black-eyed Susans.

A rain garden filled with native plants that enjoy wet conditions.

Twinleaf in the Woodland Walk.

The adorable seed pod of twinleaf looks like Kermit the Frog and always makes me smile.

opulifolius 'Tiny Wine'®), bush honeysuckle (*Diervilla lonicera* 'Kodiak® Orange'), and red-osier dogwood (*Cornus stolonifera* 'Arctic Fire® Red'). Ninebark has interesting spring blooms; it has purple-red leaves all season. I love it for its interesting peeling bark. Bush honeysuckle has brilliant orange foliage in fall. Its blooms are a pretty yellow. Red-osier dogwood has stunning dark red stems in winter. I planted mine where I can see it from my kitchen window.

The brilliant red stems of red-osier dogwood are stunning in winter and early spring.

Some Native Shrubs in My Cottage Garden

Educate yourself about plants native to your area. (A plant native to Arizona may not be appropriate for a garden in Pennsylvania.) Obtain reliable, unbiased information from university or government publications and websites. Visit native plant nurseries and preserves to get ideas. Then, use native plants in your garden, knowing you are preserving biodiversity, enhancing the livability of your home, and ensuring a legacy for generations to come.

The lovely blooms of bush honeysuckle.

Ninebark has appealing spring blooms.

I would love a meadow at the front of the house but it is too close to the road.

A meadow does not need chemicals or gas-guzzling mowers.

A Cottage Meadow Garden

Years before meadow gardens were in vogue, I wished for one at Astolat Farm. We were invited to the home of my husband's school friend to attend a beautiful outdoor wedding. Next to the house was an uncultivated field, unusual in this intensive farming area. I was drawn to the lovely grassy area, abundant with cow parsley (*Anthriscus sylvestris*), butterfly weed, and other wildflowers. It was buzzing with pollinators. It reminded me of the English village's lanes, verges, and meadows where I played as a child. (In those days, it was safe for children to roam the lanes when our parents sent us outside to play.) I would pick bunches of daisies (*Bellis perennis*), harebells (*Campanula rotundifolia*), bachelor's button (*Centaurea cyanus*), and cuckoo flower (*Cardamine pratensis*) that my mother called milkmaids. Recalling those childhood times, I decided to create my own meadow, especially as a wildflower meadow demonstrates many elements of a cottage garden. Both are loose, informal spaces with a riot of flowers. In fact, your whole cottage garden could be in the style of a meadow or a prairie. My son and his family live in the Midwest state of Iowa, where prairie gardens are popular. Prairies, like meadows, contain native wildflowers and grasses. Prairies, however, usually contain many more grasses. The French word for "meadow" is "prairie."

I would love a meadow in the front yard, but our 1840s farmhouse was built almost on the edge of the road, as was typical back then, giving me little space to garden. It wasn't until the last of my miniature horses passed away that I found the perfect spot for my meadow. The horses' pasture was the ideal size for me to manage, with a fence (protection from marauding deer)

Meadows have many elements of a cottage garden. I decided to create my own.

and eight hours of sunlight each day. I pictured a space full of buzzing and fluttering pollinators and a gazebo where I could relax and enjoy the flowers and wildlife or serve tea to my friends.

HOW MEADOWS REDUCE POLLUTION

Unlike lawn grass, a meadow does not need chemicals or gas-guzzling mowers; it requires less maintenance and water. A meadow is inexpensive to create. Therefore, a meadow is perfect for replacing some of the lawn that covers your property. You don't need to remove all of your lawn; leave some grassy areas for outdoor activities. I cut flower beds out of the lawn areas and use the remaining turfgrass as pathways between the beds.

MEADOWS BRING BACK THE POLLINATORS

As well as being a perfect cottage garden, a meadow is the ultimate pollinator garden; it contains mainly native plants to support the native insect population. A diverse range of insects—from butterflies to beetles—thrives in my meadow. There is undisputed evidence, however, that insect numbers are on the decline. When switching on the porch light after dark, I notice fewer moths and other insects fluttering around the lamp. We tend to think of honey bees and monarch butterflies when we discuss essential pollinators, but in Pennsylvania alone there are 437 species of bees; their numbers, however, are decreasing. A global decline in all insect species is a strong reason for installing a meadow on your property.

Some Insects in My Meadow

Here are a few of the many insects I see in my meadow:

Silver-spotted skipper on purple coneflower.

A tiny mint moth on lance-leaved coreopsis (Coreopsis lanceolata).

Boxelder bug on daisy fleabane (Erigeron annuus).

There is a birdhouse on each fence post around the meadow giving the birds shelter and a place to raise their young.

The bluebirds drawn to my meadow are my favorite birds.

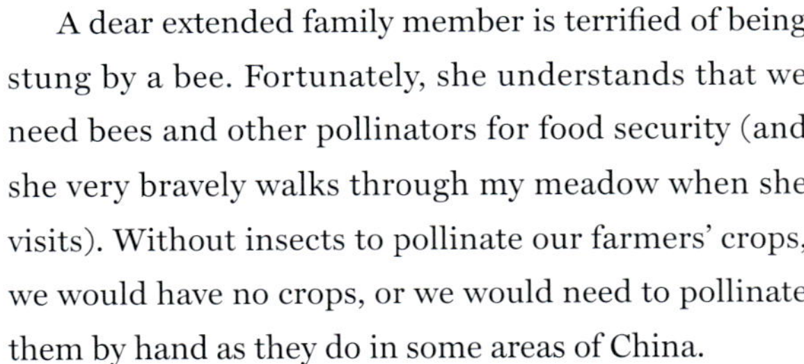

A dear extended family member is terrified of being stung by a bee. Fortunately, she understands that we need bees and other pollinators for food security (and she very bravely walks through my meadow when she visits). Without insects to pollinate our farmers' crops, we would have no crops, or we would need to pollinate them by hand as they do in some areas of China.

I love to watch the birds in my meadow. My husband fixed a birdhouse to each fence post to provide shelter for them. The bluebirds are my favorite. We need insects not only to pollinate but also for birds and other creatures to feed their young. A garden without birdsong is unimaginable, yet it could happen if we continually destroy their habitat and use chemical sprays to kill their food supply. Rachel Carson's *Silent Spring*, published in 1962, outlines this scenario. Her argument for banning DDT had the desired effect, and legislation was passed. But more has to be done. A natural meadow is one answer, providing the pollution-free habitat insects need.

One of the advantages of meadow gardens is they need little weeding once established. I must admit, the first year, I spent time removing an abundance of noxious and invasive horseweed (*Erigeron canadensis*). However, I have become much more tolerant of weeds, especially in the meadow garden. Many native butterflies and moths require a specific plant to complete their life cycles, and the particular plant they need may be one we call a weed. I planted rue (*Ruta graveolens*) not to be confused with meadow rue (*Thalictrum aquilegiifolium*). Rue, an herb, is the host plant for swallowtail and

Long-legged fly on rue.

Rue is the host plant for the swallowtail butterfly.

Show gardens at the Chelsea Flower Show are now more informal than in previous years.

other butterflies. Meadow rue can attract butterflies to eat the nectar of its flowers but butterflies lay their eggs on rue so it is a preferred plant for a meadow.

In the meadow's second year, daisy fleabane was abundant. It is considered an invasive weed. However, it is the host plant for the lynx flower moth, which can be found throughout most of the United States east of the Rocky Mountains. These plants are pollinated by a variety of bees, flies, wasps, small butterflies, and other insects. I decided not to cut down all of them. At a recent Chelsea Flower Show in London, I noticed the show gardens were looser, more informal, and quite messy—trends that pollinators love.

Growing plants that provide food for nocturnal insects, such as moths, is essential. Moths are more efficient pollinators than bees, according to researchers at the University of Sussex, England. They recommend protecting them from light pollution and planting white flowers. I light the gazebo with tea lights so as not to disturb those efficient pollinators in my meadow when we sit out there after dark. I also have white Queen Anne's lace (*Daucus carota*) in my meadow garden.

I located my meadow in a previous horse pasture.

PROCEDURE

I used a five-step procedure for making my meadow garden:

1. Choose a location.
2. Prepare the land.
3. Select the seeds.
4. Sow the seeds.
5. Manage my beautiful new space.

Instead of, or as well as, seeds, you may use starts, sometimes called plugs. Starts are seedlings, baby plants, that you purchase ready for planting.

Choose a Location

I located my meadow in a previous horse pasture that no longer served a purpose. My husband was mowing it, and therefore, creating pollution. Its gentle slope helps with drainage. Don't worry too much about the type of soil because most meadow plants are hardy in various conditions, but, of course, you will not choose an area where nothing will grow. Check with local ordinances first if you want to transform your front yard. Some homeowner associations have specific rules about what you can plant and where. One homeowner association in a Maryland community told a couple to remove their meadow and return it to lawn turf. They fought back in court and won. As a result, the state of Maryland was the first to pass an environmental law preventing homeowner associations from stopping residents from

Covering a layer of cardboard with mulch and leaving it alone for a season is an environmentally friendly way to smother turfgrass.

establishing meadows. Other states and localities are enacting pollinator-friendly laws.

Once you have chosen your location, note how many hours of sun it receives. Full sun (more than six hours each day) is best, but several meadow plants thrive in part shade.

Prepare the Land

There are a few methods of removing turfgrass (or, in my case, pasture grass): using newspaper or cardboard to smother, plastic to solarize, or an herbicide. The latter was not an option for me because it pollutes. The most environmentally friendly method is to smother it with several layers of newspaper or a layer of cardboard. Cover the cardboard with mulch and leave it for a growing season. When you are ready to plant, rake off the mulch and any remaining bits of newspaper or cardboard. I have used this smothering method very successfully in small areas of 75 to 100 square feet (7 to 9 sq. m).

My pasture field was too large for cardboard so I solarized it with black plastic. This method is not completely environmentally friendly, but is a better option, in my opinion, than using chemicals. At the end of summer, I rolled out the plastic to cover the grass and kept it in place with gardening staples. I removed it in spring. If you are sowing or planting in autumn, begin the solarizing process at the start of summer.

During this time, I had a big birthday with a zero on the end. My family and friends surprised me with money to purchase a gazebo for my new meadow. My husband

The gazebo and cairn are precisely what I wanted for the new meadow.

found the perfect one. It was not new but looked fantastic when restored and painted.

I had one other aspiration—a cairn. From the Scottish Gaelic, a cairn is a human-made pile (or stack) of stones. Cairns are found all over England, Scotland, and other parts of the world, often built as navigational aids, memorials, or landmarks. I desired one simply because it reminded me of home. A friend who works well with rocks built the perfect cairn in the meadow area.

Select the Seeds

I designed and planned the meadow through the winter months; one of the best parts of winter is shopping for seeds—online or from catalogs. One option is to purchase a packaged or canned meadow mix, but these mixes are predominantly annual seeds. They grow rapidly the first year but generally need to be replanted every year. They may also contain aggressive or non-native species. It is best to find a reputable seed merchant who sells quality seed and advises on those that will succeed in your environment. Your local conservation district is an excellent place to start for information. I used Ernst Conservation Seeds, a supplier in the Northeast. Before contacting the company, I explored their website (Ernstseed.com), where they answered most of my questions. When I eventually called them, I already knew what I needed.

A knowledgeable member of the Ernst team asked me questions about my location, the site, elevation, soil, and sunlight. She asked what I envisioned for my meadow. I told her I wanted a wildflower meadow with few grasses

The restored gazebo is perfect.

because the meadow must have a cottage garden look. Knowing it takes three years for some plants to bloom, I told her I would like a few annual seeds (for instant gratification) plus perennial and biennial ones. She advised a specific native pollinator seed mix, suitable for my location and climate. The mix included purple coneflower, partridge pea (*Chamaecrista fasciculata*), lance-leaved coreopsis, golden Alexanders (*Zizia aurea*), heath aster (*Aster pilosus*), and many other plants native to Pennsylvania. She added the annual seeds I requested: rocket larkspur (*Consolida ajacis*), bachelor's button, and sulphur cosmos (*Cosmos sulphureus*).

Sow the Seeds and/or Plant Starts

If you live in an area with mild winters, hot summers, and no frosts or freezes, seeds are most successful when you sow them in fall. Your meadow will bloom through winter, then go dormant with summer's extreme heat. In cold winter regions, you may sow in spring or fall. I chose spring.

With the help of a friend, I started the sowing process by loosening the soil's surface a little with a manual rotary cultivator—a small wheel with spikes at the end of a long handle—walking it all over the area. With a meadow, as with all gardens, you should not disturb the soil too much because tilling destroys the natural food web, harming the soil's natural ecosystem.

I placed the meadow garden seed in a bowl and added some sand (five parts sand to one part seed) before spreading the mixture by hand over the soil. Use a simple handheld spreader if you wish. I spread half over the whole region first, then changed direction and applied the other half. There is no need to cover the seed with soil. To ensure the seed made good contact with the soil, I rolled the whole meadow with a lawn roller. You can place cardboard on top of the seed for a small area and walk over it. Water the area thoroughly, using a sprinkler for a large meadow, and keep it watered well to aid germination. Germination should begin in two to three weeks.

Flowers Grown from Seed in My Meadow

The annual flowers and the perennial *Rudbeckia* provided an incredible show the first year. A local artist, Tricia Lowrey Lippert, asked if she could paint my meadow. I was delighted to agree, and equally so when my husband commissioned her to paint a picture for me. The exquisite result has pride of place in my Garden Room.

Purple coneflower, penstemon (*Penstemon digitalis*), also known as foxglove beardtongue, heliopsis, wild bergamot (*Monarda fistulosa*), and asters appeared the second year. With them came some weeds, daisy fleabane, and Queen Anne's lace, which were very pretty. I do not want them to take over so I removed many, but not all.

My husband commissioned this stunning painting, by Tricia Lowrey Lippert, of my meadow's first year.

Purple coneflower

False sunflower

Bachelor's button, also known as cornflower.

Lance-leaved coreopsis

We welcomed local artist Tricia Lowrey Lippert into the meadow throughout its first summer.

Rocket larkspur

A lot of pretty white daisy fleabane appeared the second year. I removed some as it is an aggressive spreader.

Black-eyed Susan and the annual flowers of rocket larkspur, bachelor's button, and sulphur cosmos were amazing the first year.

Heliopsis, wild bergamot, and purple coneflower in the meadow's second year.

More Flowers Grown from Seed in My Meadow

If you desire faster results, use starts as well as seeds. This is a more expensive option, of course, and more work. Purchase the starts from a reputable nursery, if possible one that specializes in native plants. Plant these little plugs well before the first frost to give their roots a chance to develop, or wait until spring. If using starts, you can make a design plan first, but keep it simple—you want that cottage garden look of abundance. I used plugs to fill in gaps I identified before the end of the first season.

Meadow Management

Little maintenance is needed once the plants are well established, except for some weeding in the first few years. I do not pull out the weeds by their roots because this method brings more weed seeds to the surface. I cut the weeds to the ground, and if there are several in one spot, I smother the weedy area with cardboard. The meadow won't look fabulous initially, and you may have difficulty distinguishing meadow plants from weeds. Investing in a plant identification app for your phone is a good idea. Take a picture of the plant in question, and the app will identify it. Or purchase an ID book. This will help you avoid removing the wrong plant.

Leave the plants standing through winter. Some people don't like how this looks, but you must leave the seeds for the wildlife. Also, the standing plants provide protection for pollinators. Since having a meadow, I have come to appreciate the beauty of standing seeds of every variety, especially when touched with frost or snow or full of twittering goldfinches.

Black-eyed Susan

Foxglove beardtongue

Wild bergamot

The meadow garden's look of abundance.

New England aster

Stokes' aster (Stokesia laevis)

In spring, it is usual to mow down a grass meadow. If you leave tall plants standing through winter in a wildflower meadow, as I recommend, you will need to cut them down in spring. I found the easiest way is to use a scythe. A scythe does not cause pollution. Use the chop and drop method to return nutrients to the soil, support soil life, and save time and energy. Chop and drop is exactly what it sounds like: Chop, or cut, the plant and drop it on the ground. This method mimics nature where fall leaves and dead plant material simply fall to the ground, decompose, and feed the soil. I cut up taller stems, such as sunflowers, with a hori hori knife in other parts of my garden, but usually one chop is sufficient in the meadow. I prefer to chop and drop in spring during or after the spring rains but you can do it in fall. It is best to wait for precipitation.

Soon, the meadow is alive once more with pollinators, and I imagine I am back in the English wildflower meadow where I played as a child.

Standing seeds have a special beauty in the fall meadow.

Goldfinches love to eat the seeds of the purple coneflower.

The early spring meadow after chop and drop. New plants are appearing.

My beautiful meadow in its third year.

Heavy snow can harm my miniature trees.

CHAPTER 4

Withstand Extreme Weather

. . . viewing the future as a climate adventure, a time of huge uncertainties but with lots of scope for positive change

—ALAN HEEKS

I like the notion of a climate adventure. However, it is not always easy to have an adventurous or confident attitude amid a heavy rainstorm, during a drought, or when the garden is enveloped in smoke during wildfire season. Despite this, you can make some positive changes and additions to the cottage garden to lessen the effects of these crises. For those areas of the country where excessive rain has been occurring frequently, a rain garden goes a long way toward mitigating the adverse effects of too much water. I will show you how to make one. In many areas, drought has become the norm. I describe steps for making the garden more drought resistant, including some suitable plants. The chapter concludes with practical steps to create fire-resistant zones to protect the cottage garden from wildfires. Gardening can be a grand adventure.

There are six rain barrels at Astolat Farm, including this one capturing stormwater from the tractor shed.

In this location, stormwater comes from the roofs of nearby houses, runs down a bank, and travels to the nearest creek or stream.

A Rain Garden in the Cottage Garden

During unpredictable weather events, I frequently find myself singing, "Rain, rain, go away . . ." from an English nursery rhyme appropriate for rainy days in England during my childhood. The weather is erratic these days, giving us wet and dry years. Wet years bring precipitation that is often very heavy; when it rains, it pours, so to speak. A 1-inch (2.5 cm) rainfall on an acre can produce more than 27,000 gallons (102,206 l) of water. Extreme weather of all types can be detrimental to your flower and vegetable gardens. We will look at specific consequences to plants and consider steps to minimize the impact.

PRECIPITATION

Precipitation, manifested by rain, freezing rain, sleet or ice pellets, snowfall, and hail, is an environmental factor influencing plant growth. Water is essential to all life and is needed for healthy plant development. Water enters a plant's stem and travels up to its leaves, where photosynthesis occurs. Photosynthesis is the process by which plants manufacture food in the form of sugar. Without water, plant cells become damaged, and plants fail to grow as they become deprived of nutrients. Too much water, however, injures plants, compacts soil, and leads to erosion. Root loss occurs when excess water reduces oxygen in the soil. A plant cannot grow without healthy roots. Extreme summer rain can leach nitrogen out of

Gaps between flagstones allow rainwater to be absorbed on paths and patios.

After a heavy rain, the Serenity Garden area flooded.

the soil; nitrogen is vital for photosynthesis. Snow provides moisture and protects plants from fluctuations in temperature. I have several miniature trees around the pond in the cottage garden; heavy snow can harm small-scale and larger trees when its weight breaks branches. Ice, hail, and deicing salts injure plants. As a side effect, deicing salts potentially lead to stormwater pollution.

Stormwater

The land where you garden is part of a watershed. Stormwater from your property drains off roofs to the nearest creek or stream and eventually goes to a larger body of water. (Our Pennsylvania land is part of the Chesapeake Bay watershed.) Stormwater picks up pollutants and carries them to its destination, potentially affecting drinking water. My home has a private well. A water test showed it was polluted, which caused us to install an expensive purification system. In addition to spreading pollution, too much stormwater can lead to flooding, damaging land and structures, and causing safety issues.

HOW TO MINIMIZE HARMFUL RAIN EFFECTS

Some ways you can lessen the detrimental effects of rain include installing rain barrels, creating a meadow (meadows are better than lawns at absorbing water), and avoiding hard surfaces on driveways and patios by using pervious pavers. Pervious pavers store water in their base until it soaks into the ground; they look like traditional pavers and come in many attractive designs. I made a patio and paths of flagstones with spaces between them to absorb the rainwater.

I am sad when I discover broken and damaged flowers after an unusually heavy rainfall, often with high winds. Damage will likely happen to tall plantings like delphiniums, foxgloves, and hollyhocks. Prevention is the best option; therefore, I stake tall flowers when I learn that a storm is coming.

If you begin with selecting native plants, you will find they often fare best because they are more likely to adapt to local conditions. Choose plants that are more resistant to fungal disease and pests; the information will be on the label. You may hear them referred to as resilient plants. When looking for resilient plants, you can get ideas from gardens that are doing well in your neighborhood. At the end of the growing season, I review which plants were successful in my garden. I have to be careful that I don't have a knee-jerk reaction to failing ones because the weather may change next year, and the plant may revive. I list plants that are doing well and eliminate ones that repeatedly fail.

Make wise choices when buying trees and shrubs. Don't choose trees with inherent weak wood or shallow roots, such as willows (*Salix* spp.). Willows are fast-growing but weak-wooded, therefore susceptible to damage in storms. They lose branches or even topple over when stressed by wind, ice, or snow. When my husband was a boy, he played beneath a Northern catalpa tree (*Catalpa speciosa*), a native of our area but inherently weak-wooded and with a brittle branch structure. He loved that tree, and I came to love it, too, despite its untidy disposition. Its large, heart-shaped leaves and orchid-like flowers made up for the messy litter made by bean-like pods when they fell. The catalpa thrived in our clay soil

Stake tall plants such as foxgloves when a storm is in the forecast.

Heavy rain and strong winds may cause damage to your plants if you do not take precautions.

We planted a dawn redwood in the wet area.

As the Serenity Garden was subject to flooding, I used the lasagna garden method of raised beds there.

A rain garden solves the problem of heavy rain accumulating on a compacted lawn.

I located a rain garden in a cottage garden border.

We used a backhoe to make the deepest depression in my small rain garden.

until we began to experience heavy rains. The catalpa prefers a well-drained site, but the location of our tree was not well drained; with heavy rains, there would be standing water. An arborist diagnosed rotting roots, and we removed the catalpa. The good news is we replaced it with a tree that has thrived because it loves standing water. The dawn redwood (*Metasequoia glyptostroboides*) is also native and fast-growing but flourishes in swamps; it is the perfect example of the right plant, right place, a handsome tree, with a bonus of beautiful fall color. We no longer see standing water in the Serenity Garden where the former catalpa reigned (no pun intended).

If your garden is recovering from severe flooding, give your land a chance to recover by installing raised beds filled with a soil mix or making a lasagna garden (I discuss these methods in the sections on sustainable gardening [page 58] and vegetable gardening [page 126]). I created raised flower beds using the lasagna method in the Serenity Garden, the area with standing water where the catalpa lived and died. Raised beds provide better drainage than conventional beds during heavy rainstorms. Also, I amend the soil in all of my gardens with organic material to help with drainage. I made a rain garden. It has proved to be an effective antidote to heavy precipitation.

WHAT IS A RAIN GARDEN?

A rain garden is a bowl-shaped garden, sometimes called an infiltration basin, designed to capture stormwater runoff and allow it to infiltrate the soil slowly. You plant rain gardens with perennials, grasses, and shrubs that tolerate wet and dry conditions. The plants transpire water, releasing it into the atmosphere and helping remove pollutants. If sited and constructed correctly, water infiltrates within one to two days and does not sustain mosquitos. A rain garden is an excellent solution to heavy rain that runs off your roofs, driveways, walkways, and compacted lawn area. Rain gardens soak up up to 30 percent more water than an equivalent patch of lawn.

I located my rain garden in a cottage garden border. I wanted to integrate it into the rest of the landscape rather than have it stand alone. I chose that spot because, although it wasn't constantly wet, it received stormwater runoff from the house gutters through an underground pipe. Stormwater would flood that particular flower bed, making it difficult for plants to survive, even though I chose plants that tolerate wet conditions. So, I removed the plants and started over.

The deepest depression in the rain garden is for plants that can tolerate standing water.

HOW TO CONSTRUCT A RAIN GARDEN

The first step for installing a rain garden is to examine your situation to determine where your stormwater runs off the house and where it goes. You may direct the stormwater from the gutter with a plastic pipe. Place your rain garden at least 10 feet (3 m) from the house in an area that is not constantly wet. Avoid septic systems. Before you dig, call your local authority to locate underground utility lines and check local laws. Test for soil permeability with this simple test: Dig a hole 6 inches (15.2 cm) deep. Fill the hole with water and check it after twenty-four hours. If the hole still contains water, you must amend the soil to remedy the slow infiltration. After you have dug out your rain garden and before planting, add 2 to 3 inches (5 to 7.6 cm) of compost and work it into the first few inches of topsoil.

My rain garden is small (under 100 square feet, or 9.2 sq. m). Because we have clay soil that seemingly grows rocks, we enlisted the help of a friend with a backhoe to dig a basin. If you don't have a friend with a backhoe, search for a local landscaper to do the work. If your soil is easier to dig than mine, you may make the basin yourself with a sharp shovel. Or you could purchase a trenching or drain spade with a long, narrow scoop, curved sides, and a sharp edge. These tools are designed to make it easier for you to dig deep into hard soil. You will find them at one of the big box stores.

Make a shallow depression by removing the topsoil. Loosen the subsoil and dig depths below the ground from 1 to 6 inches (2.5 to 15.2 cm). You should make three levels of basin-like depressions. The lowest level/deepest depression is for plants that can tolerate wetter conditions; a medium-deep depression is for plants that survive in occasional standing water; and the least

The rain garden with Joe Pye's pink blossoms invites pollinators to visit.

deep depression is for plants that prefer drier conditions. Return the topsoil and amend with compost or decayed leaves, especially if you have clay soil like mine that could be better for drainage.

Next comes the fun part: choosing plants. I went to my favorite native plant nursery, and they helped me pick out the best ones for my new rain garden. Joe Pye weed (*Eutrochium maculatum*) was my first choice.

BEST PLANTS FOR RAIN GARDENS

With cottage garden style in mind, selecting plants with various shapes, colors, and bloom times will benefit pollinators better. Of course, you will use the right plant and right place rule. Rain gardens are suitable for most locations if you choose the right plants for the area. However, a rain garden may not be ideal in a rocky area where rain runs overland. Choose native plants suitable for your new garden's dry and wet areas. There are numerous resources on the web with plant lists. The best sites are those of the university Extensions for your area. For example, Washington State University Extension has a comprehensive site dealing with Northwest rural stormwater. The Chicago Botanical Garden site has excellent information for resources in the Midwest. I suggest rain garden plants for my Pennsylvania area and North America's coastal California Mediterranean climate zone. My rain garden is partly sun and partly shaded due to its proximity to a crabapple tree. Some of the plants I chose are:

Plant copper iris in Zone 1, the wettest zone, of the rain garden.

*Swamp milkweed in the wettest part of the rain garden. Arkansas bluestar (*Amsonia hubrichtii*), located in the wet zone, and Joe Pye weed are in the background.*

The rain garden in springtime.

Zone 1: Wettest Conditions

- Swamp milkweed
- Sprengel's sedge (*Carex sprengelii*)
- Joe Pye weed
- Copper iris (*Iris fulva*)
- Blue flag (*Iris versicolor*)
- Cardinal flower (*Lobelia cardinalis*)
- Allegheny monkeyflower (*Mimulus ringens*)

Zone 2: Wet Conditions

- Arkansas bluestar
- Eastern bluestar (*Amsonia tabernaemontana*)
- Butterfly weed
- Marsh marigold (*Caltha palustris*)
- Rose mallow (*Hibiscus moscheutos*)

Zone 3: Drier Conditions

- Turtlehead (*Chelone glabra*)
- Pink turtlehead (*Chelone lyonii*)
- Threadleaf tickseed (*Coreopsis verticillata*)
- Sensitive fern (*Onoclea sensibilis*)
- Cinnamon fern (*Osmunda cinnamomea*)
- Garden phlox
- Obedient plant (*Physostegia virginiana*); note that obedient plant is really not very obedient and can be aggressive in some areas
- Little blue stem (*Schizachyrium scoparium*)

North America's Mediterranean climate zone, including California, southern Oregon, and part of western Nevada, has very little rain for half the year. It is best to have plants in these areas that can tolerate dry summers. Again, native plants are the most adaptable. Some suggestions:

Zone 1: Wettest Conditions

- Yerba mansa *(Anemopsis californica)*; note that Yerba mansa can be aggressive
- Wild ginger (*Asarum caudatum*) will take shade
- Torrent sedge (*Carex nudata*)
- Douglas iris (*Iris douglasiana*)

Zone 2: Wet Conditions

- Palm sedge (*Carex muskingumensis*)
- Yerba buena (*Clinopodium douglasii*) will take shade
- Saltgrass (*Distichlis spicata*)
- Southwestern spiny rush (*Juncus acutus*)
- Wood rose (*Rosa gymnocarpa*)

Zone 3: Drier Conditions

- Common yarrow (*Achillea millefolium*)
- Ceanothus (*Ceanothus* spp.)
- California fuchsia (*Epilobium canum*)
- California polypody fern (*Polypodium californicum*)
- Cleveland sage, blue (*Salvia clevelandii*)
- Hummingbird sage (*Salvia spathacea*)

The yellow blooms of threadleaf tickseed are seen at the front of the rain garden where the conditions are drier.

Sensitive fern is one of several types of fern in the rain garden.

Plants for Rain Gardens in North America's Mediterranean Climate Zone

Enjoy your new garden as part of the overall garden design. Your rain garden should not stand alone but should be colorful and incorporate elements of the cottage garden. For cohesion, continue the water theme in other areas by adding fountains, birdbaths, or a pond with a waterfall.

Wild ginger

Palm sedge

Yarrow

Ceanothus

I love to see the American swallowtail butterfly on Joe Pye weed when it blooms in late summer.

I have a chair under the crabapple tree from which to watch the pollinators at work in the rain garden. I love to see the American swallowtails on Joe Pye.

Creating a Drought-Tolerant Cottage Garden

As a child, I believed it rained considerably in every part of England; I was unaware that the flat areas of East Anglia were more often arid and windy. There, Beth Chatto created her groundbreaking gravel garden in the 1960s. I don't much care for the term gravel garden as it conjures up a dull picture, but Chatto used plants tolerant of dry periods that would look equally as colorful in a cottage garden. She describes the blooms in her June garden in a letter to Christopher Lloyd, ". . . the Gravel Garden in spite of the long drought, looks magnificent: the drought-tolerant plants, alliums, foxtail lilies, helianthemums, tall woolly verbascums, honey-scented clouds of crambe, soft blue catmint, and still weaving thro' it all, the electric green of euphorbias." (Chatto and Lloyd 1998) Their delightful book of published letters, *Dear Friend and Gardener*, is inspirational. Chatto shows it is possible to create a cottage garden resistant to the ravages of the extreme dryness that global warming has since brought to many more places.

USEFUL HINTS

Here are ten practices you can pursue during a drought or if you live in a region that is naturally dry for long periods. I mentioned some of these strategies when describing gardening sustainably. Still, they merit further discussion through the lens of gardening in dry conditions.

1. Reduce lawn size. I can't say this often enough. Lawns require large amounts of water.
2. Mow less frequently. According to the University of New Hampshire's Earth Systems Research Center, this small step considerably reduces carbon emissions and storage, influencing extreme weather events.
3. Allow the lawn to go dormant. It is crucial to stop mowing altogether during a lengthy drought, allowing your lawn to go dormant.
4. Use compost and mulch. I make compost and use it liberally to amend the clay soil in my garden. I spread a few inches of mushroom compost on all of my gardens in spring to increase fertility and help water drain to the plants' roots. This excellent practice works well in sandy soils, too. But do not add compost if you garden in arid regions using native and desert plants adapted to the local soils. Organic materials may cause these plants to rot. Instead, backfill the planting hole with the existing soil, then spread gravel as mulch. In gravel gardens in more temperate regions, you may use a little compost at planting time to get the roots going, or add a mixture of chicken grit, the native soil, and leaf mold. Chicken grit is a finely ground hard substance given to chickens to aid their digestion; find it at your local farm store. Mix these ingredients in a wheelbarrow and add a little to each hole as you plant.

   Use gravel, an inorganic mulch, in the dry garden. Inorganic mulches are as beneficial as organic mulches: They provide moisture retention, temperature moderation, and prevent compaction. Gravel is a mix of course rock or

A gravel garden's plants may be as colorful as those in a cottage garden.

mineral fragments sourced from quarries. I use pea gravel as a mulch because it is small and has a smooth finish. I also like small-size river stones, especially our local Pocono River stones, with their gray and red color blends. Gravel or stones should be smaller than ½ inch (1.2 cm) for weed control and drainage. I chose a ³⁄₈ inch (0.9 cm) river stone. Remember, gravel and stone are not a source of nutrients so it is crucial to monitor your plants for signs of nutrient deficiency and fertilize when necessary.

5. Install rain barrels, if permitted in your area. Water is a precious commodity in drought conditions so collecting and storing rainwater is especially important if you live in a dry area.
6. Water early in the morning before the day's heat causes fast evaporation. If the mornings do not work for you, an evening watering is appropriate. Plant in groups, placing those plants with similar watering needs together.
7. Irrigate wisely. Choose a method of watering that you like: drip irrigation, soaker hose, or watering can. Remember to apply water to the root area, not spray from above.
8. Minimize the number of container plantings. Containers dry out faster than garden beds so limiting the number is wise in drought conditions. Potted plants for shade require less watering.
9. Add water features.
10. Choose resilient plants tolerant of dry periods and plant them in a gravel garden.

In the following segments, I elaborate on the last two suggestions.

Plants thrive in gravel when you use chicken grit, the native soil, and leaf mold to get the roots going at planting time.

*Small-size river rock looks attractive in my dry garden. In this area I planted artemisia (*Artemisia schmidtiana*).*

WATER FEATURES

Water features are essential to my cottage garden, providing sound, movement, wildlife, stress relief, and beauty. They also have a special place in the dry garden and during drought conditions. Unfortunately, some believe that when a drought hits, they should drain the water from these features, but there is no need because the water is recycled. Furthermore, insects and other wildlife need water; providing some during dry periods helps them survive.

During hot weather, water cools as it evaporates. Too much evaporation, for example, from a tiered fountain that splashes, does not conserve water as you attempt to keep it filled. Tall fountains are also vulnerable to wind

Water features have a special place in the dry garden.

A pond covered with water lilies provides minimum exposure of water, thus reduces evaporation.

The pretty cutleaf maple shading the waterfall significantly cuts down on evaporation.

The temperature in the woodland garden is 10 degrees cooler on a hot day than other parts of the property.

drift, which causes faster evaporation. A better option is a simple birdbath placed in the shade, allowing for slower evaporation. The goal is to make your cottage garden into a cool oasis.

Choose water-wise features such as a bubbling fountain that has little spray. There should be minimum exposed areas of water; for example, cover a pond with water lilies (*Nymphaea* spp.) to reduce evaporation. Some water lilies are hardy in zones 3 through 11. My pond has a waterfall shaded by a dwarf cutleaf maple (*Acer palmatum*); the pretty maple significantly reduces evaporation. Birdbaths should be as deep as possible because shallow water heats up quickly and evaporates fast.

You should not use chemicals to keep the water clean; they defeat the purpose of having a pollutant-free garden. Pond water will not develop algae if you install a simple skimmer, a type of mechanical filter. When placed at the pond's edge, the water passes through a net, basket, or screen to capture debris.

Two more hints: Fill your water feature in the early morning and use mosquito dunks if you are worried about mosquitos. Mosquito dunks are small, donut-shaped, floatable larvicide disks that dissolve in water and kill mosquito larvae.

Remember these attributes when choosing your cottage-style water feature—whether a pond, pondless

waterfall, fountain, or birdbath. A water feature in a natural material like stone is best to keep the look of a cottage garden. Surround it with a simple planting of long-blooming perennials.

PLANTS FOR DRY AREAS

My garden has experienced spells of drought lasting several weeks as the summer months are now bringing higher temperatures to my area. My plantings help alleviate this problem. We know that plants, especially trees, provide cooling through shading. On a hot day, I like to walk in my woodland garden, where the temperature is as much as 10 degrees cooler than other places. My husband planted a grapevine that covers a pergola on our small deck, providing a cooler place to sit outdoors.

Research for the Royal Horticultural Society in the United Kingdom shows that certain plants help cool the environment with shade, reflection, and a process within their cells that converts water to water vapor. The latter process consumes heat from the air, leading to ambient cooling. Examples of plants the researchers found to have these traits are salvia (*Salvia* spp.), lamb's ear (*Stachys byzantina*), and heuchera (*Heuchera* spp.).

Plants for dry areas often have gray and silver leaves that reflect the heat. Leaves tend to be small to reduce the area of evaporation and may have a waxy cuticle, a layer of wax that minimizes water loss and provides added protection. Some plants have in-rolled leaves to protect the stomata, the microscopic pores on leaf surfaces. All of them tend to have extensive root systems that are circular in shape to allow for quick absorption of water when it rains, or they have taproots that extend very deep into the ground.

Grasses, such as prairie dropseed (*Sporobolus heterolepis*), are an appropriate choice to add to a gravel garden. However, don't plant too many grasses if you want to keep the cottage garden look. I love self-sowing plants like poppy (*Papaver*). You can start them by sprinkling the seeds over the gravel in early spring. My list of plants for dry areas includes:

- Yarrow
- Aeonium (*Aeonium* 'Cyclops')
- Allium (*Allium*)
- Artemisia
- Baptisia (*Baptisia* 'Ivory Towers')
- Bougainvillea (*Bougainvillea* cv.)
- Calamint (*Calamintha nepeta*)
- Echeveria (*Echeveria* spp.)
- Pale purple coneflower (*Echinacea pallida*)
- Prairie baby's breath (*Euphorbia corollata*)
- Fennel (*Foeniculum vulgare*)
- Catmint
- Poppy
- Foxglove beardtongue

The grapevine covering the pergola over the deck provides a cool oasis on a hot day.

- Jerusalem sage (*Phlomis russeliana*)
- Caucasian sedum (*Sedum spurium*)
- Prairie dropseed
- Thyme (*Thymus vulgaris*)
- Yucca (*Yucca filamentosa*)

Many of the plants on my list are native to the United States. I include two herbs, fennel and thyme, both of which need little supplemental water. In the tradition of a cottage garden planting, I like to include some herbs or vegetables among my flowers.

Heuchera and shady trees cool the environment.

FAVORITE PLANTS FOR THE GRAVEL GARDEN

*Yarrow (*Achillea millefolium *'Saucy Seduction')*

Drumstick allium loves the gravel garden's dry conditions and reminds me of a good friend and of a beloved grandson who has grown into a professional drummer.

*The pearl yarrow (*Achillea ptarmica *'The Pearl')*

I also chose lavender (*Lavandula* spp.) for the gravel garden but this short-lived plant survived for two to three years only. I decided not to replace it, even though the bees and I loved it, but you should try to grow it.

It is important to me to evoke memories or make new memories with my plantings. I planted drumstick allium for my grandson, Harry, when he began playing drums. Additionally, this plant reminds me of a good friend, Katharine, who gave me the plant.

Lavender likes full sun and well-drained soil, so you may want to grow this beautiful plant in your dry garden.

Purple bougainvillea (Bougainvillea)

Variegated yucca (Yucca gloriosa *'Variegata'*)

Bronze fennel

Hens and chicks (Sempervivum tectorum)

Red poppy (Papaver somniferum)

Yellow wild indigo (Baptisia sphaerocarpa) *with allium*

My gravel garden is in a sunny spot, facing south. It is next to the rain garden.

The gravel garden at Chanticleer Garden in Wayne, Pennsylvania.

CREATING A GRAVEL GARDEN

For inspiration, I visited the gravel garden at Chanticleer Garden in Wayne, Pennsylvania; Beth Chatto's garden in Essex, England, is still on my bucket list. I returned home from Chanticleer excited about the plants they grew there and eager to start my new venture.

I chose a location in full sun. The spot should be level or slightly sloping. I picked a border with good drainage. It is close to my rain garden, which drains adequately, and has an overflow pipe carrying excess water well away from the flower bed, so I wasn't worried about flooding. (Placing my dry garden next to a rain garden is a testimony to the rain garden's efficiency.) I ordered gravel to be delivered from my favorite garden supply center and removed most existing plants to prepare the bed, leaving just a few daffodil bulbs. I did not excavate, but you may take off the top layer of soil to level it, and add some grit and compost to the soil. I had a wheelbarrow nearby with the planting mixture described in the compost and mulch section. The border had an edging of rocks, and I made it a little higher before adding 2 to 3 inches (5 to 7.6 cm) of gravel. I placed a few larger rocks around the area; I liked how they looked.

I purchased plants in pint-size pots for easy planting, placing them on top of the gravel in the new garden and moving them around to create the desired effect. Space your plants according to the recommendations on the plant label.

Planting is different in a gravel garden. I pushed away some gravel for each plant and made a hole in

When the plants fill out, the gravel garden will look like the cottage garden but require less work.

the soil below, pouring water into it. Before placing the plant in the hole, I removed as much of the potting mix as possible from the plant's roots, teasing the root ball until most of the potting mix fell off. This method also removes weed seeds from the roots. Place the plant's roots in the hole, spreading them out carefully. Cover the roots with your homemade planting mixture before pushing the gravel around the plant. Avoid getting soil in the gravel because it may block the air space between particles. The plant's crown should be flush with or slightly below the top of the gravel.

It is vital to keep the plants watered well until they become established. Check them daily, and water them deeply at the roots when necessary. Putting a soaker hose in place around the plants will lighten the task.

Once the plants are established, your gravel garden needs little maintenance. Cut the plants back in spring, pull the occasional weed, and top up the gravel if needed. You will rarely need to water. Eventually, the plants will fill out, and the garden's colorful plantings will look like the rest of your beautiful cottage garden but with less work.

Your gravel garden will succeed due to placing your chosen plants in the place that gives them the conditions they need to thrive. Chatto coined the mantra of all successful gardeners: right plant, right place. Today, gardeners across continents are installing gravel gardens in response to the warmer climate. Beth Chatto died in 2018, aged 94, leaving an enduring legacy for gardeners throughout the world.

A Fire-Wise Cottage Garden

I gave wildfires little thought except for feeling sorry for Californians and other people in fire-prone areas. I prayed for their safety as I watched firefighters on the nightly news battle dramatic flames. My complacency was shattered in summer 2023 when my garden became blanketed with an unhealthy smoky haze from wildfires in Canada. At first, we didn't know the cause of the otherworldly orange haze; after all, Canada is almost 600 miles (965 km) from my home in the Pocono Mountains of Pennsylvania. The smoke affected 75 million people, from the Midwest to the Northeast, stuck in a weather pattern of high pressure that led to winds bringing the smoke out of the north. I quickly understood that I could not work in my garden during this unhealthy event, with the smoke affecting my breathing. If I had to go outside, I wore a mask.

SMOKE AND ASH IN THE GARDEN

I was concerned about the effect of smoke and ash on my plants. Scientifically, smoke contains toxic levels of nitrous oxide, sulfur dioxide, and ozone that reduce photosynthesis. Photosynthesis is the process by which green plants use sunlight to make food from carbon dioxide and water. Reduced photosynthesis impedes plant growth, lessens fruit production, and slows ripening. Over time, smoke can affect the taste of fruits and vegetables. To mitigate these effects, as soon as it was safe to go outside, I watered the plants well, hosed down their leaves with a gentle spray, and applied fish emulsion fertilizer to the soil to promote healthy roots. If you experience smoke and ash on your fruits and vegetables, rinse them well outdoors and again in the kitchen sink. Peel off the skins of tomatoes, apples, and other fruits, and remove the outer leaves of leafy greens. Wear a mask, wash your hands afterward, and be careful not to track ash indoors. If a structure fire caused the ash or you have any concerns, throw the produce out. Some studies say washing the affected vegetables is sufficient, others say it is safe to compost them, but if in doubt, throw them out.

Although dealing with the new (for me) phenomenon of smoke, I felt fortunate to live in an area of the United States that is least affected by wildfires. Debris burning was traditionally Pennsylvania's leading cause of wildfires due to homeowners ignoring burning bans issued by local authorities. The fires would often start in backyards and travel into bordering woodlands. In fall 2024, the reality of the imminent threat from wildfires struck home with the Blue Mountain wildfire only 15 miles (24 km) from our home. Hundreds of local and state firefighters worked for seven days to contain the raging wildfire. Nearly 600 acres (242.8 ha) were scorched. At that time, we were experiencing extremely dry conditions with no rainfall for several weeks, and drought was declared in half of Pennsylvania's counties. We watched the local news anxiously until the fires were extinguished. I couldn't help but feel concerned for the future and for our little farm, which has 15 acres (6 ha) of woodland.

As increased hot and dry conditions lead to more wildfire events, we should all know how to make firewise gardens. I ask my gardening friends in the North American West to forgive me for preaching to the choir; the following information is critical for newbie gardeners as wildfires become more common.

If you have smoke and ash on your plants, water them well and hose down their leaves with a gentle spray.

You should not have densely planted flower beds like these around your house if you live in an area affected by wildfires, but there are some cottage garden elements you can apply.

Many grasses, such as fountain and feather grasses, are highly combustible.

The crabapple tree is deciduous and fire resistant.

FIRE-WISE GARDEN DESIGN AND PRACTICES

Wildfires only occur if there is fuel to burn. Ground-level objects such as grasses, leaf litter, mulch, and small plants act as fuel, carrying the flames, if they are hot enough, into shrubs, low branches, and tree canopies. Dwellings catch fire when flames, radiant heat, or airborne embers (the most common cause) ignite fences and decks that abut them. Creating a 5-foot (1.5 m) ember-resistant area around the home reduces the risk. Remove flammable decks, fences, hedges, and mulches, and use pavers, decorative rock, or pea gravel for paths and patios. If you keep your deck, paint it with fire retardant, frequently rake out leaves and other debris from underneath, or enclose the open area beneath with ⅛-inch (0.3 cm) metal screening to block embers. You should remove trellises, climbing plants, and tall shrubs against the house. Relocate log piles, compost piles, fuel tanks, sheds, and lawn furniture to an area at least 30 feet (9.1 m) from the dwelling. Within 30 feet (9.1 m) of your home, cut down dead trees and trim the branches of mature trees. Thin the trees so their crowns are at least 18 feet (5.5 m) apart. Remove shrubs, vines, and Spanish moss.

Plant your flower beds between 5 feet (1.5 m) and 30 feet (9.1 m) from your house. While any plant will burn, consider choosing fire-resistant ones that are less likely to combust. Regularly water, prune, and maintain them by removing dead foliage and keeping them debris-free. While you may plant small shrubs in clumps, place large ones individually. Spacing your plants and adding paths and rocks is crucial to prevent fire from spreading.

With fire-wise design, you will not be able to have the same lush, densely planted flower beds, and indeed not around your house, but there are some aspects of the cottage garden you can apply. Your garden will look different from the conventional cottage garden, but it will still be charming and easy to love.

FIRE-WISE PLANTS

Any plant can burn given the right conditions, but some are more flammable than others, especially those containing oil, resin, wax, and sticky sap. My gardening friend Dee Nash experienced the 2023 Simpson wildfire in Oklahoma. While her home survived, most of the surrounding neighborhood burned. Dee urges you to remove Eastern red cedar trees (*Juniperus virginiana*) or any other high-resin junipers near your house. They contain cedar oil that ignites rapidly and sends out sparks and cinders at great distances. Cedar trees have become invasive in Oklahoma. Native plants are not less flammable than non-native ones, but non-natives often spread rapidly and outcompete native plants. Many grasses, such as fountain and feather grasses, are considered highly combustible, especially when there is heat and drought and they are allowed to dry out. Invasive grasses fueled the deadly 2023 wildfires in Hawaii. Other plants to avoid are fine-needled evergreen trees and shrubs and trees with peeling bark.

Fire-resistant plants have an open, loose branching form and little dead wood or foliage. Their leaves are broad, flat, and supple with high moisture content. They are not resinous or waxy and contain little oil. Fire-resistant trees have fewer branches and are slow growing; deciduous trees, for example, crabapple and dogwood, are best. The leaves of succulents, such as sedums, are filled with water. Some groundcovers, like moss phlox (*Phlox subulata*), are slow to burn.

Deadnettle with creeping Jenny (Lysimachia nummularia *'Aurea'*)

Moss phlox

Hens and chicks

Stonecrop groundcover

Here are several suggestions for fire-resistant plants suitable for a cottage garden:

Groundcovers

- Pussytoes (*Antennaria* spp.)
- Rock cress (*Aubrieta deltoidea*)
- Basket of gold (*Aurinia saxatilis*)
- Poppy mallow (*Callirhoe involucrata*)
- Iceplant (*Delosperma* spp.)
- Sulphur buckwheat (*Eriogonum umbellatum*)
- Deadnettle (*Lamium* spp.)
- Moss phlox
- Stonecrop (*Sedum* spp.)
- Hens and chicks

Purple coneflower

Delphinium

Daylily

Bearded iris

Bergenia

Perennials

- Yarrow (*Achillea* spp.)
- Hummingbird mint (*Agastache* spp.)
- Ornamental onion (*Allium* spp.)
- Columbine (*Aquilegia* spp.)
- Butterfly weed
- Bergenia (*Bergenia cordifolia*)
- Mariposa lily (*Calochortus* spp.)

Mock orange

Serviceberry

- Delphinium
- Coneflower
- California fuchsia
- Daylily (*Hemerocallis* spp.)
- Sedum 'Autumn Joy' (*Hylotelephium* 'Herbstfreude'), previously known as *Sedum spectabile* 'Autumn Joy'
- Bearded iris (*Iris ×germanica*)
- Lavender
- Prickly pear cactus (*Opuntia* spp.)
- Prairie coneflower (*Ratibida columnifera*)

Blue mist spirea

Shrubs

- Serviceberry (*Amelanchier* spp.)
- Blue mist spirea (*Caryopteris ×clandonensis*)
- Kelsey dogwood (*Cornus sericea* 'Kelseyi')
- Mock orange (*Philadelphus* spp.)
- Shrubby cinquefoil (*Potentilla fruticosa*)
- Western azalea (*Rhododendron occidentale*)
- Compact American cranberrybush viburnum (*Viburnum trilobum* 'Compactum')

Shrubby cinquefoil

The stunning Mariposa lily is native to western North America.

I love the look of gravel and rocks between plants.

PUTTING IT ALL TOGETHER

To create a cottage garden in a location prone to wildfires is not an impossible challenge. Of course, you cannot plant densely or close to your house in this environment. Still, many other elements of cottage garden style are possible, such as creating wide, curvy borders, using an informal plan, and choosing a mixture of plant types. Edge your borders with one of the groundcovers listed, remembering to space the plants. Your garden will be a riot of color with traditional cottage garden plants such as purple lavender, yellow coreopsis, white allium, and blue delphinium. It will be extra enjoyable with the addition of plants native to hotter climes, such as the Mariposa lily.

I love the look of gravel and rocks between plants and have that effect in my gravel garden. Remember to add a focal point: a beautiful statue, a water feature, or an interesting shrub. Include a small patio of brick or pavers and add a chair made from fireproof material. One element of the traditional cottage garden is to have very little lawn. You do not need a lawn in this type of garden—save your precious water for the flower beds; keeping your plants hydrated is critical to keeping them fire resistant.

Being realistic, we know that fire-wise gardening is not fireproofing. However, you can make a difference by creating spaces that interrupt a fire's path and by removing possible fuel sources. Sit on your patio with a cool drink and enjoy watching the pollinators visiting your beautiful fire-resistant cottage garden.

I located my vegetable garden in an area receiving full sun. We added the fence later.

CHAPTER 5

Stock the Pantry

It's difficult to think anything but pleasant thoughts while eating a homegrown tomato.

—LEWIS GRIZZARD

High food price inflation in the United States peaked at 11.3 percent in 2022 during the COVID-19 pandemic, according to Purdue University's Joseph Balagtas, professor of agricultural economics. Since that time, even with inflation down, grocery prices continue to strain consumer budgets significantly. As mentioned earlier, growing your food is a valid solution to this problem, and we can go a step further and share extra produce with those experiencing food insecurity. In this chapter, I describe how to accomplish all of this, plus offer hints on companion planting, a technique of growing different plants together to benefit each other. Companion planting is an important element of the cottage garden style.

I grow my victory garden using the square foot gardening method.

Growing Vegetables in the Cottage Garden

Bloom where you are planted, a popular gardening slogan found on T-shirts and mugs, describes precisely what we were asked to do during the COVID-19 crisis. I translated the catchphrase into "stay home and garden." At that time, 18 million new gardeners were born; maybe you were one of them. If so, you found that growing vegetables saves a ton of money. That's not all; your garden makes our planet healthier because producing and transporting food to the grocery store uses more water than growing your own and has a high carbon cost. In addition, store-bought food is not as fresh and requires more packaging. If you garden organically, you also have the satisfaction of knowing you are not consuming chemicals. Nothing is better than eating a freshly picked tomato bursting with flavor straight from the vine.

The coronavirus pandemic led to numerous features and blog posts suggesting you start a victory garden; however, few authors detailed how to do it. I will provide a victory garden how-to for the beginner and describe square foot gardening, my favorite vegetable growing method. I will also explain the importance of rotating crops, give hints on growing herbs, and discuss growing vegetables in containers for those with little space.

THE NEW VICTORY GARDEN

My husband's mother, Constance Hubbard, was honored for her victory garden. During the Second World War, while my father-in-law was away serving in the US Army, she planted a victory garden, answering the government's call to grow vegetables to increase food production. The victory garden was a practical way to contribute to the war effort. At the time, she lived in New Brunswick, New Jersey, where she worked for Johnson & Johnson. The company published a picture of Constance in her victory garden on the cover of their *Bulletin* magazine and wrote a brief article describing her work at the company and praising her for her garden. They said, "Her Victory Garden is miraculously free of weeds because of her constant and excellent care. She has beans, peppers, cabbage, lettuce, corn, beets, potatoes and radishes."

Connie spent her childhood on a farm. After the war, she purchased Astolat Farm, where she raised her two children. My husband, Duane, never moved away;

I moved there after our marriage in 1988. Connie continued growing a vegetable garden into her eighties, riding the big field tractor to cultivate between the rows. She never allowed Duane to do this task since he drove over her seedlings when he was young. As she aged, we became increasingly afraid she would fall off the tractor so, finally, my husband removed the wire to the tractor coil so the engine wouldn't start for her.

James H. Burdett, the founder of the National Garden Bureau, wrote the *Victory Garden Manual* in 1943. It is out of print now, but many of his recommendations still apply and have influenced my gardening methods. Nowadays, you are more likely to see the term homesteading, especially on social media, but I prefer victory garden—a victory over the virus during the COVID-19 pandemic and an ongoing victory over high food prices.

Here are my step-by-step instructions for creating a new victory garden:

One zucchini plant produces enough for my husband and me, with extra for donating.

1. Decide where to locate your vegetable garden. When deciding where to put the garden, pick the sunniest spot possible. Vegetables will be most productive in full sun, meaning they should receive six to eight hours of direct sunlight daily. If you have only shade, try lettuce, radishes, spinach, and Swiss chard; I have grown beets in part shade. Locate the garden near a water source and, if possible, near the kitchen door for easy access.
2. Determine the size. You can grow staple crops in a 10 by 10-foot (3 by 3 m) or 12 by 12-foot (3.6 by 3.6 m) area. You can always make it more extensive next year. Your garden can be any shape; mark it off with a water hose or string.
3. Remove the sod. Sod removal is the hardest part. Keeping a flat-bladed spade parallel to the ground, slice through the top 1 to 2 inches (2.5 to 5 cm) of sod and soil. Turn it over, place it next to the garden, and leave it to dry and kill the roots. After removing all the sod, spread 1 inch (2.5 cm) of compost over the soil. Next, push a garden fork into the ground and rock it back and forth to loosen the subsoil, promoting improved movement of air, water, roots, and soil organisms. When the sod that you removed is dead, spread it over the bed with any topsoil and mix it all in. Mulch your vegetable garden as soon as possible to prevent weeds. Newspaper wetted

Rhubarb plants return every year for early rhubarb pies.

Plant your garden by sowing seeds directly or use bedding plants.

down makes a suitable mulch. Just slice a hole or slit through it when you are ready to plant.

We increasingly understand the importance of disturbing the soil as little as possible. Soil contains microfauna necessary for the soil and crops to be healthy. Consequently, do not use a rototiller. Add a layer of compost at the beginning of each gardening season to aid aeration and drainage, preventing the soil from becoming compacted.

4. Choose which plants to grow. Make a list of your family's favorite vegetables. Include some unique crops, such as heritage varieties, that you can't find in the supermarket. When deciding how many plants you need, consider how much produce your family can consume at harvest time. For example, one zucchini plant may be enough as each plant is prolific. Having a reasonably small kitchen garden, I grow a variety of crops in small numbers.

   Some plants in the vegetable garden, such as rhubarb, grow for more than one season. Consider growing rhubarb if you have enough space. I like rhubarb because it can be harvested earlier than most other vegetables. A rhubarb pie is very welcome after the long winter months.

5. Explore where to find seeds and plants. Purchase seeds from online merchants; browsing seed catalogs during winter months is a favorite pastime of most gardeners. When reading seed catalogs, look for the words "broad disease resistance" and "widely adapted plants"; it should also say something about the quality of the vegetable. I prefer to use organically produced seeds. Order bedding

I like to display the seed packets in my potting shed when I have finished sowing.

You may sow lettuce before the last average frost date because it favors growing in cool weather.

plants from nurseries online or visit local garden centers. To ensure success, it is best to purchase from merchants as near to your location as possible. Plants grown in California, for example, may not thrive in Pennsylvania.

6. Plant your garden. There are two planting methods: directly sowing seeds or using bedding plants. I direct sow seeds of beans, beets, carrot, cucumbers, kale, lettuce, peas, radish, spinach, squash, and Swiss chard. I prefer bedding plants for basil, broccoli, cabbage, cauliflower, eggplant, peppers, and tomatoes. You can grow some of the bedding plants indoors from seed or purchase them from a nursery if you are a beginner gardener. Plant garlic, onions, potatoes, and rhubarb from bulbs, tubers, or roots.

7. Follow suggested sowing and planting dates. Direct sow your seeds outdoors following the suggested times on the seed packets. For example, some crops, such as lettuce, peas, and spinach, favor growing when the weather is cool so you may sow them before the last average frost. Sow those seeds that prefer warm weather after the last frost date. Search for the last frost date for your area online or by contacting your local Extension office. Follow the instructions on the seed packet for depth and spacing. Plant bedding plants when the danger of frost has passed. After covering the seeds with soil or nestling the plant's roots into the ground, put the mulch back in place and water the plants or seeds well.

OUR FAVORITE VEGETABLES

Fennel

Snow peas

Broccolini

Cherry tomatoes

GROWING VEGETABLES IN A SMALL SPACE

Don't fret if you're short on space for the type of victory garden I describe. Container gardening is a fantastic solution. It's not just a practical alternative to traditional gardening, but also a visually appealing one. Imagine having a garden on your patio, balcony, deck, or porch, with pots, baskets, boxes, or barrels filled with your favorite flowers and vegetables. The benefits are numerous: You have control over the soil composition and can move the pots to optimize weather conditions, showcase unique plants, and transform your space's entire look.

When it comes to containers, you have a wide range of options: clay, concrete, fiberglass, metal, plastic, terra cotta, or wood. You can even repurpose items like buckets, milk jugs, ice cream containers, bushel baskets (lined with perforated plastic), barrels, dishpans, or trash cans. However, keep in mind that all containers must be clean, nontoxic, and have at least one drainage hole. The size of the containers will vary, but most vegetables need at least 6 to 8 inches (15.2 to 20.3 cm) for adequate root growth. I find containers that hold at least 2 gallons (7.5 l) of soil work best.

Remember, small pots dry out quickly and can blow over in windy weather, whereas large containers can be heavy to move. Consider using dollies or plant caddies (platforms with wheels). Placing plastic saucers under your pots or using self-watering containers will prevent water stains on your patio or deck. Elevating your planters slightly helps the drainage holes work correctly.

Good growing mixes provide essential plant nutrients, hold adequate moisture, and allow excess water to drain. There are two types of growing media: those that contain soil and those that don't. Never use soil straight from your garden as it may contain too much clay. Clay holds moisture when wet, blocking air from the plants' roots. You may use high-quality packaged potting soil formulated for vegetables from the local garden center. Soilless mixes are usually too light for vegetables; you could mix them with 25 percent soil. Be aware that garden soil may contain insects, weed seeds, or diseases. I make my own growing medium with one part potting mix, one part garden loam, and one part perlite.

You can grow most annual vegetables in containers except sweet corn because numerous plants are needed for adequate pollination. Also, vining crops like squash, pumpkins, and melons require more space. Some new cultivars are suitable for containers: bush-type squash, cucumbers, and melons grow as compact bushes rather than sprawling vines. When choosing tomatoes, look for determinate cultivars that grow to a predetermined height. Indeterminate tomatoes grow too tall.

Here are examples of vegetables, container size, and spacing:

- Plants for a ½-gallon (1.8 l) container:
  Beets planted 2 to 3 inches (5 to 7.6 cm) apart, and Swiss chard or lettuce planted 4 to 6 inches (10.1 to 15.2 cm) apart.
- In a 1-gallon (3.7 l) container, plant 1 cherry tomato.
- In 2-gallon (7.5 l) containers, plant bush beans 2 to 3 inches (5 to 7.6 cm) apart or bell peppers, 1 plant per container.
- In 5-gallon (18.9 l) containers, plant cabbage 12 to 18 inches (30.5 to 45.7 cm) apart or cucumbers

An attractive container garden of vegetables on a deck.

spaced 14 to 18 inches (35.5 to 45.7 cm) apart; plant 1 eggplant, summer squash, or tomato plant.

Planting in containers is a straightforward process anyone can master. Start by covering the hole in the bottom of the planter to prevent soil from clogging it, then add your chosen growing media. Fill the container about half or three-quarters full, set your transplants on the mix, and add more potting media until it's about an inch (2.5 cm) below the rim. Sow seeds and plant transplants according to the depth and spacing instructions on the seed packet or tag. Place your container in a spot that gets the right amount of sunlight for your plants and water thoroughly. It's that simple!

Caring for Your Container Garden

Follow these tips to grow almost anything grown in the ground in a container:

- Soil in containers can dry out very quickly so check them at least once a day and water as necessary. Do not allow the media to become completely dry. Apply water until it runs out of the drainage hole.
- Fertilize with fish emulsion every couple of weeks at the dilution recommended on the bottle. If you purchase a soil mix with added fertilizer, you won't need to do this for eight to ten weeks.
- Check vegetables periodically for insects and diseases. Remove pests by hand or with a strong

You can grow vegetables in a planting box in any sunny spot, even in a city lot.

spray of water if they are aphids. Use organic insecticidal spray if necessary. Remove damaged or infected leaves to prevent the spreading of the disease. Remove and destroy the whole plant if severely infected. Clear the area around the plant.

- Shelter your containers in severe weather and protect them from early fall frosts. I use bubble wrap around the container as insulation.

- Harvest vegetables when ripe so the plant will continue to set more fruit.

SQUARE FOOT (METER) GARDENING

Would you like to grow abundant fresh vegetables in a small space with less weeding, no tilling, no heavy digging or removing the sod, and less work? If so, I recommend you try square foot (meter) gardening. Mel Bartholomew introduced this intensive gardening method in America in 1981, and today gardeners worldwide practice his successful system. He introduced it to British gardeners with his 2013 book, *Square Metre Gardening: The Radical Approach to Gardening that Really Works* (Cool Springs Press), adapted from his highly successful *All New Square Foot Gardening*, which updated his 1981 American edition. Typically, in America you use a 4 by 4–foot planting box, fill it with soil, and place a square-foot grid on top to create sixteen squares. For gardeners in England, Bartholomew recommends a 3 by 3-foot (about 1 by 1 m) planting box with a grid of nine squares. Plant seeds or bedding plants in the squares created by the grid. This alternative to traditional row gardens has many advantages: You harvest more vegetables by planting them in blocks instead of rows. There are fewer weeds because you dedicate every square to vegetables. Your existing soil's quality doesn't matter. The soil stays friable, not getting compacted, because you never walk on the squares. There is no tilling. These gardens warm faster and drain better than traditional gardens. You won't waste water. You can grow vegetables in any sunny spot, even in a city lot. Taller raised beds spare your back and allow seniors and people with disabilities to enjoy gardening.

Here is the detailed seven-step procedure. I will use the term "square foot gardening"; you may substitute square meter gardening if you wish. *Note that 1 square foot is equal to 1 square meter when discussing the measurement of materials.*

1. BUY OR BUILD A BOX. Find suitable boxes in the big box stores or online. Purchase them made from rot-resistant cedar boards or synthetic wood, both popular options. You can put them together easily without tools. Six inches (15.2 cm) is deep enough because almost all vegetable roots grow in the soil's top 6 inches (15.2 cm). Place one box on top of another to double the depth if you wish to grow deeper-rooted vegetables such as parsnips. The boxes will last many years; they can be relatively expensive but are worth the initial investment for all the advantages square foot gardening offers.

   If you prefer, build your boxes or elicit the services of a handyman, as I did. Make the boxes with any nontreated lumber—the chemicals from treated lumber may leach into the garden soil. Have the boards cut into 4-foot (about 1 m) lengths at the lumber yard. Designs can differ; for example, my boxes are 4 feet wide (about 1 m) and 8 feet (about 2 m) long. While the length is not significant, make your box, at most, 4 feet (about 1 m) wide, or you won't be able to reach the middle when you garden. Drill holes in the ends of the boards and screw them together with 3-inch (7.6 cm) screws. You can paint the boards with outdoor house paint to last many years.

2. CHOOSE A LOCATION. Remember, when locating your square foot garden, vegetables will be most productive in full sun. Place the garden near a water source and, if possible, near the kitchen door, as mentioned previously. If you place your square foot garden on the grass or a weedy area, put corrugated cardboard or four layers of newspaper on the bottom to discourage grass and weeds from growing into the garden. Do not use plastic because it does not allow water to soak through. When utilizing more than one box, place them 3 to 4 feet (0.9 to 1.2 m) apart to make a walkway and enough room to push a wheelbarrow between them.

3. FILL THE BOX WITH POTTING SOIL. Bartholomew advises you to use one-third blended compost, one-third peat moss, and one-third vermiculite. As peat moss is not environmentally friendly, I substitute coir, coconut fiber, to create

Taller raised beds let seniors and people with disabilities enjoy gardening.

Buy or build a box for your square foot garden.

In a 4 by 8-foot (1.2 by 2.4 m) planting box two 4 by 4-foot (1.2 by 1.2 m) grids placed end to end divide the box into thirty-two 1-foot (about 1 m) squares.

a well-drained soil with enough moisture and nutrients for plant growth. Blended compost means compost of different types. I mix mushroom compost, aged horse manure, and homemade compost. Compare ingredients on compost bags at garden centers and purchase a variety; or find the products at the big box stores or your farm store. I mix the components in a wheelbarrow before tipping them into the box.

4. **ADD A GRID.** The grid is the unique feature of this system; with it, it is a square foot (sq. m) garden. Make a grid from wood, plastic strips, old window blind slats, etc. Use screws to attach them where they cross. When using a 4 by 4-foot (1.2 by 1.2 m) planting box, the grid should divide it into sixteen squares. Premade grids are also available online.

5. **START PLANTING.** The square foot gardening method is less wasteful of seeds as little thinning is required. Read the seed packet to determine what spacing your plant needs. If the plant requires 12 inches (30.5 cm) of space, put one seed in each square, such as one broccoli, cabbage, corn, eggplant, or pepper seed. Remember, you need enough corn plants for wind pollination therefore sow a minimum of sixteen seeds—one in each square. For 6-inch (15.2 cm) spacing, plant four seeds in each square, such as four chard, lettuce, or marigold seeds. With 4-inch (10 cm) spacing, you may plant nine beet, bush bean, garlic, onion, or spinach seeds. With plants needing only 3-inch (7.6 cm) spacing, plant, for example, sixteen carrot or radish seeds. Plant

The grid is the unique feature of the square foot gardening method, as shown in this aerial picture of my garden.

one cucumber, melon, or squash in 2 square feet (0.1 sq. m). Place trellises on the north side of your planting box to grow vining plants such as beans or peas. On the north side, they won't shade other vegetables. As you can see, there is no wasted space in a square foot garden, and production is much higher.

Plant each seed by making a shallow hole with your finger. Cover the seed lightly without packing the soil. When using bedding plants, make a shallow, saucer-shaped depression where you place the plant to help direct water to the root system. Water in the mornings to prevent quick evaporation and disease; direct the water to the base of the plants. I use watering cans and rainwater, but you may install soaker hoses for easy irrigation. Mulching your garden will help retain soil moisture and suppress weeds.

6. ADD PROTECTION. It is easy to protect the square foot garden from animals using chicken wire or netting and to safeguard against too much sun with row covers, material readily available by the roll. You can purchase row covers as an all-purpose fabric that protects against chill, insect pests, and birds. Fabrics of specific weights are available for particular needs including insect pests and for protection from cold to extend the growing season. You may make supports with bent wire hangers, or buy ready-made hoops, to cover just one square or all of the garden.

Wire hoops support netting to protect the plants.

Harvest vegetables in a timely fashion.

As the growing season draws to a close, leave perennial vegetables standing.

7. **PROVIDE ONGOING CARE.** Check for the ripeness of vegetables and harvest them in a timely fashion. As each crop finishes in a square, install a new one, first adding a shovelful of new compost. At the end of the season, after a killing frost, I pull out the brown and shriveled plants, including the roots. Bean roots are an exception: Cut down the plants and leave the roots in the ground, as I explain more when discussing companion planting (page 142). Leave perennial vegetable stalks standing, such as asparagus, to provide cover for pollinating insects. More and more gardeners are allowing dead plants to compost into the soil. I rake the gardens to expose underground grubs and pupae to the sun, birds, and freezing temperatures before adding compost from my compost bin. You may plant a cover crop such as winter rye to provide nutrients. In the spring, cut it down or till it into the beds before it goes to seed.

ROTATING CROPS

With traditional row and square foot gardening, you can minimize plant diseases by rotating crops among plant families. Grouping vegetables into families and moving each family to a different location each year will help limit diseases that overwinter in the soil. Closely related plants are susceptible to the same insect and disease problems. Moving the crop family to a different location each year lessens the chance of disease. A list of the seven plant families follows:

1. Gourd: Cantaloupe, cucumber, pumpkin, squash, and watermelon
2. Mustard: Broccoli, brussels sprouts, cabbage, cauliflower, and kale

Herbs love raised beds because they drain freely. I grow mine on the patio near the kitchen.

3. Nightshade: Eggplant, okra, pepper, potato, and tomato
4. Onion: Chive, garlic, leek, and shallot
5. Pea: Bean and pea
6. Parsley: Carrot, celery, and parsnip
7. Amaranth: Beet and Swiss chard

In my larger boxes (I have four), I grow beans and peas in the first, cucumber and squash in the second, beets and Swiss chard in the third, and garlic and onions in the fourth, giving me a four-year rotation. I grow other vegetables in smaller boxes and rotate them every two or three years.

GROWING HERBS

Fresh herbs are expensive to buy in the supermarket; it makes sense to grow them yourself. Herbs love raised beds and containers because they drain freely. I have two tall planters full of herbs. I placed them on the patio to be near the grill and my kitchen door for easy picking. Basil, chives, parsley, rosemary, sage, and thyme are staples for me, and I choose other types as the fancy takes me.

I grow herbs, for example, dill, in my vegetable garden for pest control and some in my cottage garden for beauty. Of course, we must remember to grow flowers, vegetables, and herbs side by side in the cottage garden. I cover that topic in more detail in the section about companion planting (page 142).

Chocolate mint contained in a planting box.

My cold frames protect vegetable plants into the fall months and beyond.

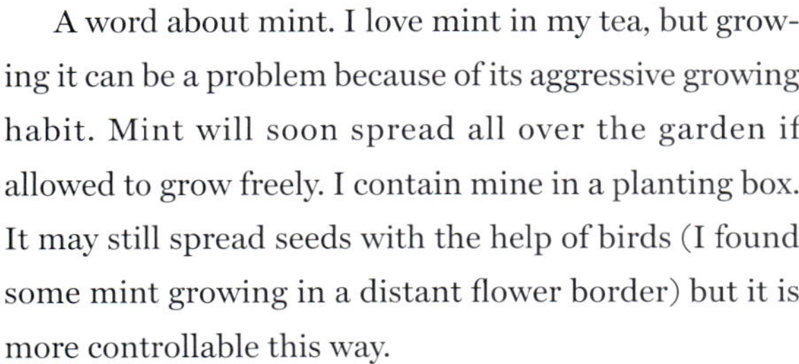

A word about mint. I love mint in my tea, but growing it can be a problem because of its aggressive growing habit. Mint will soon spread all over the garden if allowed to grow freely. I contain mine in a planting box. It may still spread seeds with the help of birds (I found some mint growing in a distant flower border) but it is more controllable this way.

EXTENDING THE GARDEN SEASON

If you are not ready to give up fresh, homegrown vegetables at summer's end, consider extending the garden season into fall. Follow these simple practices and you will have a productive garden up to and beyond the first frost. Many vegetables thrive in cooler temperatures including broccoli, brussels sprouts, cabbage, carrots, cauliflower, kale, lettuce, mustard, peas, spinach, and turnips. Row covers, cold frames, and other forms of protection for your plants make it easier to plant into fall and continue the harvest when summer concludes.

To ascertain when to begin your fall planting, determine how many days to maturity as stated on the seed packet. Count back that number of days from the average frost date, allowing an extra two weeks for the slower growth that occurs with the cooler fall weather. To speed up the process, I like to start my seeds indoors. When the sprouts are about ¼ inch (0.6 cm) high, I plant them deeper than normal in the garden so only their first leaves are showing, then water well. When deciding where to plant, you should know your garden's microclimates: Most gardens have mini areas that differ significantly from one another. For example, do you have a spot shielded from cold or wind by a fence or shrubs?

Do you have low spots where cold air and frost readily settle? Do not plant fall crops in the latter location. Successive planting is another way to stretch the garden season. Replant seeds at periodic intervals—for example, sow radishes and spinach once a week; carrots and salad greens every two weeks. Some crops, such as carrots, kale, parsnips, and spinach, may survive all winter. Many cool-weather crops, such as parsnips, not only endure but also improve in flavor after a frost. In my family, we traditionally enjoy roasted parsnips from my garden with our Christmas dinner.

To plant for a fall harvest:

- Add a light layer of compost or a small application of complete fertilizer to restore nutrients removed by previous crops before planting your fall harvest.
- To reduce pest and disease problems, never plant vegetables of the same family in the spot where they grew the previous season.
- Plant after a rain when the soil is moist, or water thoroughly the day before planting.
- Sow seeds about twice as deep as you would in spring, then cover your seeds with organic mulch such as loose straw.
- When the seedlings are up, remove the straw to allow the sun to reach them.
- When the plants are established, add a heavier mulch to conserve soil moisture and inhibit weed growth.

If you live in an area that experiences wide seasonal temperature variations, it is possible to extend your garden into early winter or longer by protecting your plants from extreme weather conditions. Apply 8 inches (20.3 cm) of mulch to overwintering crops to prevent the soil from heaving. Water when needed. When a mild frost (no lower than 30°F, or −1°C) is forecast, cover your fall crop with baskets, blankets, boxes, buckets, or burlap or canvas sacks. Structures such as cold frames, hoop houses, cloches, and floating row covers provide protection during lower temperatures. As previously mentioned, protecting vegetables can extend the growing season by several weeks.

Cloches (cloche means "bell" in French) act as mini greenhouses, raising daytime air temperatures by up to 10°F (about 5°C); the residual heat insulates the plants at night. A garden cloche is a small transparent shell placed over an individual plant. Nineteenth-century French gardeners used glass jars, which unfortunately had no ventilation. A simpler, but effective, modern version is the cut-off plastic jug—remove the cap to provide air circulation.

A floating row cover is a more elaborate version of the cloche, covering several plants at once. The covers are made of spunbonded or woven synthetic material that allows light and rain to penetrate. The fabric protects from frosts down to 28°F (−2.2°C). I use them on my raised beds, placing the fabric over a (purchased) frame. You can build a simple, inexpensive frame out of PVC piping. It is important to secure all edges of the covers so they don't blow around.

Offering a greater degree of frost protection than floating row covers, a cold frame is a bottomless box with a glass or clear plastic top (usually hinged) that lets in

I prop open the cold frame covers to prevent overheating as needed.

the sunlight and opens for ventilation. You can build a cold frame from a variety of materials such as wood or cinder blocks. Select a site with well-drained soil and orient the glass to face toward the south or southeast. I have a high-backed cold frame with the rear (north side) against a shed for wind protection. The higher back lets me grow taller crops. I place bales of straw around the base of my cold frame on very cold nights. A cold frame needs to be monitored carefully to ensure it does not overheat on sunny days. I use a thermometer and I prop open the covers with a stick when the temperature reaches 40°F (4.4°C), and I remove the covers completely when the temperature reaches 60°F (15.5°C).

A hoop house or high tunnel is a temporary structure with a metal frame covered with greenhouse plastic. The sides may be fastened to a moveable bar the gardener rolls up in the morning and down at night for ventilation and temperature control. If you use a hoop house, it is important to monitor and manage air temperature and pests. Keep in mind that hoop houses tend to be more costly.

You can also use my suggestions to start your garden earlier next spring. I grow lettuce and other cool-weather crops in my cold frame. By fall, I sometimes feel tired of taking care of the garden, but then I consider the savings in food costs. Also, there is a wonderful feeling of satisfaction from knowing you are making the most of your garden for as long as possible.

Please don't feel overwhelmed by the work and detail involved with establishing your vegetable garden. Once you begin the process, you will see that many of your cottage gardening skills readily transfer to this area. As

A hoop house is a temporary structure.

with any worthwhile project, it does take effort, but keep in mind the rewards are well worth it: You will be harvesting an abundance of fresh, homegrown vegetables for years to come.

Companion Planting

I don't remember seeing flowers and vegetables growing side by side in my grandmother's garden, except for the colorful marigolds (*Tagetes*) bordering almost every vegetable bed. Nevertheless, tradition has it that one of the elements of an English cottage garden is growing vegetables and flowers together. I love this concept and practice it in my garden.

We know that the first cottage gardens in medieval England were a mishmash of vegetables, a few herbs, and a smattering of self-sowed wildflowers. Animals, such as chickens and pigs, would complete the picture. There was little room so, by necessity, vegetables and herbs took priority to feed the family and meet their medicinal needs. Maybe the peasant's wife, spotting a pretty cowslip (*Primula veris*), a cousin of the more recent primrose, in the meadow near her cottage, dug it up and found a little space in her garden. Could that be how the tradition of growing flowers and vegetables together began?

Gardeners today have learned the merit of some tried and tested flower and vegetable combinations. We call it companion planting when two or more plants grow side by side to benefit each other. Maybe the peasant's wife knew the cowslip would attract pollinators, contributing to higher vegetable yields. Companion planting began in America as long ago as in England, when the Indigenous North Americans first planted corn, pole beans, and winter squash alongside each other—a triad known as the Three Sisters. The tall cornstalks provide living support for the beans, the beans add nitrogen to the soil, and the large squash leaves suppress weeds and give shade to help the soil stay moist.

TYPES OF COMPANION PLANTING

There are three types of companion planting: intercropping, trap cropping, and a third type when the gardener grows plants next to each other so one improves the flavor of the other or keeps pests at bay.

Intercropping, sometimes called interplanting, occurs when the gardener considers each plant's growing habit to increase yield. The Three Sisters method is a case in point. Another example is growing small plants that require shade under taller plants.

My cutting garden bed is located next to vegetable beds. The flowers attract pollinators to the vegetable plants.

Cowslips in my cottage garden

The second type of companion planting, trap cropping, occurred when the peasant's wife planted her cowslip, or when you plant colorful flowers to attract pollinators to your vegetable garden. There is some scientific evidence for the validity of intercropping and trap cropping.

The third type of companion planting, when the gardener puts plants next to each other so one improves the flavor of the other or keeps pests at bay, carries no scientific proof for its effectiveness, but my grandfather swore that dill improves the taste of cabbage when they are planted together. He also believed onions planted next to cabbages discouraged caterpillars and that marigolds are a wonder plant, deterring all pests. Research does indicate that marigolds' roots produce toxic biochemicals, destroying nematodes that can kill plants. I am sorry to say, though, that the benefits occur only when you grow marigolds as a cover crop and then till them into the bed at the end of the season. However, even without scientific evidence, I trust my grandfather's judgment and use his companion planting methods.

THE BENEFITS OF COMPANION PLANTING

The most important reason for planting a variety of crops and rotating them each year is to maximize diversity. Increasingly, agricultural crops are planted in extensive monocultures with little genetic diversity, stripping the land of nutrients and making the crops particularly susceptible to disease and insect outbreaks that ruin harvests. By increasing diversity through companion planting, you are, in a small way, helping the

My grandfather believed that onions discourage caterpillars and marigolds deter all pests.

The Three Sisters planting of corn, pole beans, and winter squash is companion planting at its best.

environment and protecting the health of plants. The plants in your garden are more vigorous when grown in a community.

With companion planting, certain plants, such as dill and fennel, attract predatory beneficial insects that eat pests, helping with pest control. As I mentioned, you promote pollination when you add flowers to your vegetable garden; they entice and keep pollinators there. Attracting pollinators is crucial with the decrease in the bee population. My husband always lures butterflies by placing a puddling dish, a shallow bowl containing a muddy mixture of sand, cow manure, and water, in the vegetable garden. Male butterflies enjoy puddling or fluttering their wings in the mix to absorb minerals. I attract birds to my vegetable garden with bird-friendly plants like sunflowers along with a birdbath. The birds eat slugs and other pests, such as aphids. They need caterpillars as food for their young.

The Three Sisters combination shows that companion planting can save space and maximize yield. Try this combination of corn, squash, and beans. We know that beans are nitrogen producers, so when you rotate your crops next year, place some nitrogen-needy plants, such as broccoli, where you grew the beans. There will be more nitrogen in the soil if you leave the beans' roots in the ground, cutting the plants at ground level when they have finished producing.

Finally, a colorful mosaic of plants adds to the beauty of your garden. Companion planting has many lovely benefits.

The plants in your garden are more vigorous when grown in a community.

Fennel attracts predatory beneficial insects that eat pests.

The cabbage white butterfly lays eggs on the nasturtiums and spares the cabbages.

PLANTS THAT WORK WELL TOGETHER

Here are some beneficial combinations for you to try in the vegetable garden:

- **Tomatoes and basil; peppers and basil.** Basil protects tomatoes by repelling flies, mosquitos, and tomato hornworms. It keeps spider mites and aphids away from peppers. Basil reportedly improves the tomato's flavor.
- **Cabbage, cauliflower, kale, and nasturtium (*Tropaeolum majus*).** The cabbage white butterfly loves to lay eggs on brassicas such as cabbage, cauliflower, and kale. The emerging caterpillars can quickly consume these vegetables. When nasturtiums are present, the cabbage white butterfly lays eggs on these plants and spares the brassicas.
- **Eggplant (aubergine) and pot marigold (*Calendula officinalis*).** Pollinating insects love calendula flowers. They will then pollinate the flowers of eggplants that are close by.
- **Carrots and spring onions.** This combination is mutually beneficial because the smell of the onions repels the destructive carrot root fly, and the smell of the carrots deters the harmful onion fly.
- **Dill and cabbage.** There is no scientific evidence that dill improves the cabbage's flavor, but try it and judge for yourself.
- **Summer savory (*Satureja hortensis*) and fava beans (broad beans).** Summer savory repels the black flies common to fava beans.

'Bright Lights' Swiss chard (foreground) is an attractive asset to any vegetable or flower garden.

- **Marigolds and nasturtium with everything.** Both flowers are easy to grow from seed—plant them with any of your vegetables to attract beneficial insects.
- **Lavender and leeks or carrots.** Lavender and oregano, with their strong aromatic leaves, deter aphids and other pests such as the allium leaf miner.

Consider planting some vegetables and herbs in the flower garden. I always plant thyme near roses as the herb's strong scent deters black flies. I plant creeping thyme (*Thymus serpyllum*) along the edges of several flower borders in my cottage garden because I like how it looks and smells. Dan Benarcik, horticulturist at Chanticleer Garden in Wayne, Pennsylvania, in his webinar,

Grow marigolds with everything.

Nasturtiums are good companions for the herbs in my patio raised planting box.

Inspiration and Combinations: Finding the Right Mix, suggests combining edibles and ornamentals. He identifies 'Bright Lights' Swiss chard (*Beta vulgaris*) and dahlias (*Dahlia* spp.) as a stunning combination for early fall. Actually, Swiss chard is an asset to any cottage garden flower bed. Another favorite vegetable of mine for the cottage garden is fennel. I plant bronze fennel in the gravel garden where it thrives in dry conditions and provides a feathery contrast to the perennial flowers.

PLANTS THAT SHOULD NOT BE TOGETHER

Some plants make poor companions. It is not advisable to grow plants from the same family together. They are less likely to share infestations from pests and diseases when you distance them from each other if you have a large enough garden. In my small, square foot gardening space, I do not have the luxury of keeping them apart; fortunately I have yet to have a problem.

Here are some plant enemies:

- Carrot and dill. Dill makes the flavor of carrots stronger and the texture woodier. Carrots cause dill to be milder and have weaker stems.
- Peas and beans with garlic, onions, or chives. Garlic, onions, and chives stunt the growth of beans and peas.
- Potatoes and cucumbers. Cucumbers may encourage blight in the potatoes.
- Radishes and chervil (French parsley). Be aware that chervil makes radishes hot; you may or may not want this, depending on your taste.

There are few precise scientific studies about companion planting. There are, however, numerous anecdotal accounts. Your observations over time will authenticate which combinations work for you.

A FEW MORE TIPS

To maximize space in your vegetable garden, try relay sowing. When you direct sow seeds, stagger their installation. I sow seeds in half the squares in a bed, and two weeks later, I sow the rest. This method extends the supply of vegetables as all the plants do not mature at once. You are also less likely to get a glut of a particular vegetable. I practice relay sowing with bush beans, red beets, and Swiss chard, but it will work with any of your favorite crops.

Succession planting is a strategy for using space created when you harvest mature plants. Begin this early in spring by planting cool-season crops such as lettuce and spinach; when you harvest them, fill the vacant spots with other vegetables such as tomatoes and peppers. I do this with snow peas, planting a crop of beans in their place when the pea plants have finished producing.

Plant fast growers, like radishes, between slow-growing crops such as cucumbers or squash. You will harvest the radishes before the cucumbers need the space. As well as being a space saver, the fast-growing vegetable helps retain water in the soil and keep down weeds.

Growing vegetables in pots or other containers is the way to go if you garden on a small patio or balcony. You can even companion plant in pots. Experiment and have fun!

Sharing the Bounty

GROW FRESH FOOD TO SHARE

I will always be amazed at the enormous number of zucchini one plant produces. You must have heard the joke about gardeners who creep outside under cover of darkness and leave their extra zucchini on neighbors' doorsteps. I know one neighborhood where they quip that they only lock their cars during zucchini season. However, in these times of food inequality, a glut of vegetables is not bad. Vegetable gardeners are known for their generosity and can help people who are food insecure in several ways. Community outreach such as Plant a Row (PAR) and other programs make contributing easy.

PAR, sometimes called Plant a Row for the Hungry, is a national initiative encouraging backyard gardeners and farmers to plant an extra row of vegetables and donate their harvest to local food banks and food pantries. The University of Delaware aptly describes the program as people helping people, one pound at a time, one row at a time. GardenComm, formerly Garden Writers Association, an organization of garden communicators, launched PAR in 1995. Former director Jeff Lowenfels asked readers of his garden column to plant an extra row and donate the produce to an Anchorage, Alaska, soup kitchen. PAR grew with the mission of enabling and encouraging the 70 million gardeners and farmers in the United States to help feed the 31 million (according to PAR) adults and children who go to bed hungry every night.

One plant produces an enormous number of zucchini.

Plant a Row for the Hungry (PAR) encourages gardeners to donate extra vegetables to a food bank or pantry.

There may be a garden near you devoted to growing fresh, local produce specifically for a food pantry.

The food grown for those experiencing food insecurity must be culturally relevant.

One food distribution day, I visited the food pantry at my place of worship to take some produce and was shocked to see how many people were there for donations. I had no idea there were so many food-insecure families in my area, and I am sure there must be many more than I witnessed at that time. Your one extra row of vegetables can make a difference. If you don't have space for an extra row, there may be a garden near you devoted to growing fresh, local produce specifically for a food pantry. These gardens need volunteers. In my county, The Garden of Giving is a nonprofit organization that cultivates and provides fresh eggs and produce to several local food banks. They depend upon volunteers, both children and adults, to care for the garden. I encourage you to participate in one of these ventures.

There are several other outreach programs, such as AmpleHarvest.org, a nationwide nonprofit organization. Gary Oppenheimer, a nationally recognized game changer in food waste and hunger, developed AmpleHarvest.org in 2005. AmpleHarvest uses technology to educate and enable home and community gardeners to donate their surplus harvest to food pantries. Their mission for America is to eliminate wasted food, malnutrition, and hunger in each community. AmpleHarvest.org pays particular attention to developing program models that specifically address the needs of the population being served. For example, through a network of gardening experts and in collaboration with Tribal Elders and Native American food and hunger authorities, AmpleHarvest.org established a program called AmpleHarvest.org in Indian Country, which serves Indigenous Americans in reservation settings. This food pantry model was developed to meet the needs of communities that lack traditional street addresses or zip codes and may have limited internet access, both of which may impede effective food distribution.

The hunger relief organization Feeding America is the largest charity working to end hunger in the United States through a partnership with food banks, food pantries, and local food programs. Feeding America works with the food industry to rescue food that would otherwise go to waste. During national disasters, they help communities acquire food and emergency assistance. In addition, the organization conducts research studies to learn more about food insecurity in local communities.

In addition to these critical national programs, many local organizations distribute a wide variety of nutritious food. The Feeding America network includes 200 food banks and 60,000 food pantries in nearly every community in all fifty states, Washington, DC, and Puerto Rico. The food provided to those experiencing food insecurity must be culturally relevant and reflect the food habits and preferences of the population being served. Particularly with migrant populations, effective programs are sensitive to the culture they represent.

The Garden of Giving

HOW TO DONATE FOOD

You planted an extra row and have various vegetable offerings. What do you do next? Let's look at the difference between a food bank and a food pantry, and I'll give you some donation guidelines.

A food bank collects food from regional neighbors, gardeners, retailers, grocery stores, and restaurants. They inventory and distribute the donated food to local food programs such as food pantries. Food banks are different sizes, varying from small buildings to vast warehouses. They hire drivers for their food delivery.

A food pantry is a community site that distributes food and other products directly to those experiencing hunger. Each community is different; some food pantries are in churches or schools, whereas in other places the pantries may be on wheels. Mobile pantries may distribute food in prepacked boxes or display it on folding tables for people to choose. One such mobile pantry on Long Island, New York, provides food for seniors in their community. Volunteers from some food pantries make deliveries to the homes of seniors and others. Food pantries located in hospitals and health care facilities take food to people who are currently unhoused.

DONATION GUIDELINES

The Feeding America website has a simple tool for finding your nearest foodbank or pantry. Call the pantry before making a delivery and ask about their preferred delivery days and times. Check whether they accept fresh produce and if they need the items you have; they may have already accumulated numerous bags of zucchini and can't accept more.

If possible, provide organically grown produce. If you use pesticides, always read and follow the instructions on the label. Note the time to harvest after using the pesticide. If you are unsure you followed the label's instructions properly, put the food in the landfill and do not compost, eat, or donate it.

Here are nine steps to help ensure your vegetables are suitable for donation:

1. Water your plants the day before harvesting if there is no sign of rain. Pulling root vegetables, such as beets, carrots, and parsnips, out of damp soil is easier. Water content is critical for leafy vegetables like lettuce if the recipient won't eat it the same day.
2. Wash your hands with soap and water before harvesting. Hygiene is critical. Do not harvest if you are sick.
3. Harvest vegetables early in the morning, removing dew with paper towels. Your offerings should always be freshly picked.
4. Inspect each item for severe bruising, mold, overripeness, or insect damage. Each vegetable should be of good quality.
5. Separate produce types, keeping each type in individual, clean, food-grade bags or containers.
6. Keep the produce cool once harvested because it will likely be consumed on a different day. Place vegetables in a shady area until you can refrigerate them.
7. Clean the produce of mud and dirt. Tomatoes and squash are best left for the eater to wash before consuming.
8. Handle the produce safely to minimize foodborne illness.
9. Do not donate anything you would not serve to your family.

Your donations should always be freshly picked.

Reclaiming vacant lots, previously covered with garbage and weeds, is an essential goal of city community garden projects.

The Bill Emerson Good Samaritan Food Donation Act is a federal law named for US Representative Bill Emerson (Missouri) in recognition of his support for issues relating to those who are hungry. President Bill Clinton signed it into law in 1996. The bill protects gardeners who donate food from civil and criminal liability if the product causes harm to the recipient. When you have delivered your offerings to the food pantry, feel good knowing your gardening efforts are helping someone eat without worrying about whether they can afford it. We must all work together to create a future where no one is hungry.

COMMUNITY GARDENS

Even gardeners without a vegetable garden can produce vegetables for themselves and others by working in a community garden. Your community may have garden plots available to residents. Middle Smithfield Township Community Garden Park, Monroe County, Pennsylvania, is the perfect example. Residents of the township may rent a garden plot for a low, refundable deposit. Each plot is a large, raised bed, and gardeners may reserve up to three. The community garden is entirely organic, and renters must complete a free class about organic gardening practices before planting. Penn State Extension master gardeners periodically hold courses on organic pest control, square foot gardening, encouraging pollinators, and other topics. The renters at this beautiful community garden are encouraged to donate vegetables to a local outreach program; they reserve some beds for this purpose.

Living in a large city should not deter you if you are an avid gardener. An estimated 29,000 community gardens are in the one hundred largest cities in the United States. For example, the Pennsylvania Horticultural Society (PHS) supports more than 170 community gardens in and around the city of Philadelphia.

Reclaiming vacant lots, previously covered with garbage and weeds, is an essential goal of city community garden projects. Neighborhoods deteriorated with the foreclosure of homes, increased crime, and the prevalence of dangerous abandoned buildings. Lack of access to affordable fresh, healthy foods gravely affected members of these disinvested communities. With community gardens growing an abundance of vegetables in these neighborhoods, families have a chance to fight the food crisis.

Many city community gardens set aside space to grow vegetables for community outreach programs. For example, City Harvest (run by PHS) distributes vegetables to food banks around Philadelphia. PHS joined the Philadelphia prison system to form the Roots to Re-Entry program, where inmates learn about gardening. They grow vegetable seedlings and distribute about 250,000 a year to more than one hundred community gardens and other sites in the city.

Urban gardening ventures have many advantages in addition to providing families access to fresh food and reducing grocery bills. Many older cities have combined sewer systems in which all water and toilet water go to the same place. With large amounts of rainfall, the sewer water enters and pollutes rivers and lakes. Community gardens have more permeable surfaces with soil absorbing rain, creating a healthier living environment. Finally, we must remember the social impact of gardening as a community. People of all ages, ethnicities, and abilities form deep social connections, fulfilling the need to create a united community in a divided world.

We have looked at some practical methods by which the home gardener can help families suffering from food insecurity. Volunteering in a community garden is a valuable way of sharing the bounty. It has been shown that when we help others, our own stress is greatly eased. Stress relief through gardens and gardening is the subject of the next chapter.

The Pennsylvania Horticultural Society supports more than 170 community gardens in and around the city of Philadelphia.

CHAPTER 6

Ease Stress

I know from personal experience how gardening helps heal many mental and physical ills ... When you are consumed by anxiety, it will soothe you, and when the world is a dark and bleak place, it shines a light to guide you on.

—MONTY DON

Stress can manifest in various ways, but a garden is a simple and accessible remedy. Flowers and plants have profound healing effects, whether you're actively working, sitting, or strolling in a garden. I'll define a healing garden, then outline three ways to find stress relief—by creating or visiting a healing garden, by enjoying the benefits of a sensory garden, or by delighting in a cutting garden. These types of cottage gardens are not just beautiful but also within your reach, offering a source of encouragement and motivation in the face of stress.

In the forecourt at Chanticleer Gardens in Wayne, Pennsylvania, gardeners rake the gravel daily to keep it fresh in Japanese Zen garden style.

A beautiful example of a cloister garden.

The Cottage Garden as a Healing Garden

I am a huge believer in the healing power of gardens. As a child in England, I was a victim of the influenza pandemic, known colloquially as the Asian flu. The scope of the pandemic cannot be compared with COVID-19, but an estimated 20,000 people in the United Kingdom and 80,000 citizens in the United States died from the virus. I was very ill. I remember the dreadful nightmares that I now know were caused by fever. I remember being extremely weak when my recovery began. I will never forget my first time outdoors after the fever passed. Supported on each side by my parents, I walked feebly along the garden path to a shady bench. I sat there listening to birdsong and enjoying a light autumn breeze. Sitting in the garden became a daily routine until I recovered my health completely. I credit those healing times spent in the family garden as a huge factor in my recovery. I included a healing garden in the design when I made my Pennsylvania garden.

Healing gardens are not new. Japanese Zen gardens and monastic cloister gardens began hundreds of years ago. Zen gardens started as a place for meditation in the temples of medieval Japan. The monks created them to enhance feelings of tranquility and evoke serene reflection. Zen is a Japanese translation of "Chan," a Sanskrit word meaning meditation. Through meditation and reflection, the beholder of the garden strives toward the Buddha's experience of attaining enlightenment. The gardener carefully controls the Zen garden using raked stones, rocks, and low plantings. Today, Hoichi Kurisu, president and founder of Kurisu LLC, designs

There were many visitors on the Japanese bridge at Monet's Garden when I was there. They were quiet and reflective.

Monet painted many pictures of his tranquil lily pond.

and builds innovative healing gardens throughout the United States and abroad. He built a garden at Oregon State Penitentiary, a maximum-security prison, with the inmates' help. It was built, Kurisu said, for social justice and healing, enlisting nature as an individual and systematic transformation agent. His Japanese-style healing gardens demonstrate the power of meaningful interaction with nature in daily life.

Monks created cloister gardens in medieval monasteries. Located in an open courtyard surrounded by covered walkways, the monks would pray as they worked. You can see an example of one of these gardens at the Met Cloisters, a museum in the Washington Heights neighborhood of Upper Manhattan, New York City. The museum cleverly incorporates medieval architecture into a modern building built to evoke the Middle Ages. A visit to this extraordinary museum is yet another place on my bucket list. However, I was fortunate to experience a similar garden at the high school I attended. The Friary School for Girls was established in the remains of a medieval friary in Lichfield, England. The friary was built in 1237 by Franciscan monks, an order founded by St. Francis of Assisi. When I was a student, remnants of the friars' gardens were on the school grounds; we called the area The Monk's Walk. Teachers chose senior girls to make gardens in this revered place. There, in the throes of teenage angst, I again experienced the healing power of a garden, this time from working there rather than just sitting.

Claude Monet (1840–1926), the French artist who founded Impressionist painting, created his garden at Giverny near Paris to aid his recovery from a debilitating depression. He then painted it to help heal the war-torn French nation. He said he wanted his works to

I call my healing garden the Serenity Garden.

A shady swing in my Serenity Garden is the perfect place to start my day.

have healing effects. My grandson and I visited Monet's garden on a day when it was very crowded with sightseers, yet visitors were quiet, calm, and contemplative—a testament to this garden's tranquility.

For years, there have been healing gardens at hospitals and health care facilities, providing a place of refuge for patients, families, and staff. The Secret Garden at the Ronald McDonald House in eastern Wisconsin is a beautiful example. They have communal vegetable gardens and flowers, all in a serene space. There are healing gardens attached to many cancer units in hospitals. Some are also available to veterans and others coping with post-traumatic stress. If you have a family member recovering from a serious medical condition such as cancer or stroke, or if there is an individual in your home dealing with the aftereffects of trauma, consider creating a garden that heals.

Healing gardens have many names: wellness gardens, contemplative gardens, peace gardens, prayer gardens, and meditation gardens. The church my husband and I attend, like many churches, has a prayer garden. At Astolat Farm, our home, I created a garden called Serenity, a place of refuge from the hectic pace and stresses of daily life.

There are many names, but just two distinctive types of healing gardens: restorative and enabling. A restorative garden is one in which you benefit simply by being there. Walking or sitting in the garden has restorative qualities. The enabling healing garden is one in which you gain from working in it. Home gardeners can avail themselves of both types of healing gardens. Unfortunately, you may spend much of your time weeding, planting, and pruning, allowing little time for relaxation and so losing a valuable aspect of the healing garden. I have learned the power of starting my day in a secluded area of my Serenity Garden, where I sit and read my daily devotional. Try something similar: Sit in your garden, admire the flowers, and listen to the birds. Your day will be better for it.

HOW GARDENS HEAL

Scientific evidence shows that when you connect with nature, positive changes occur in the body: lowered blood pressure, decreased heart rate, reduced stress, and improved mood. Actively working in the garden improves heart health, weight, blood pressure, cholesterol levels, and the quality of sleep. The science team of the Royal Horticultural Society (RHS) in England joined with researchers in Europe and the United States to determine how gardens affect the environment and our health. The results of these and other scientific studies show us the many healing benefits of the garden.

Research by the scientists at the RHS shows that when you increase time spent in a garden or other green space by 10 percent, you gain the health equivalent to being five years younger.

Vitamin D from the sun fights off bacteria and viruses, strengthens bones, and helps nerves transmit messages from the brain. (It is essential, however, to wear skin protection to ward off the harmful effects of the sun's rays.) Sunlight also boosts serotonin, the hormone that regulates mood, causing you to feel happier and calmer, and lowers levels of cortisol, the stress hormone. A University of Michigan study showed that twenty minutes in nature significantly reduces cortisol.

Soothing sounds and smells calm the brain, slowing the mind to a less frenetic pace. A University of Michigan study showed a reduction of ADHD symptoms with time spent outdoors in a garden.

There are helpful benefits for veterans suffering from post-traumatic stress disorder and for patients recovering from a severe illness.

Soil contains beneficial microbes, microscopic organisms that boost the immune system. Scientists found some microbes act as antibiotics. (We know penicillin came from mold, one of the many types of fungus.) I encourage you and your family to get your hands into soil. Yes, allowing little children to play in the dirt is permissible. Just have them practice proper hygiene—handwashing after the activity. Scientific studies show that children exposed to microbes in soil have a higher rate of immunity when they become adults. They also show that less contact with beneficial microbes has caused a rise in allergies and other autoimmune conditions.

Hospital patients with a window view of green spaces need fewer pain medications. At Samaritan Lebanon Community Hospital in Oregon, patients frequently turn off their televisions to view a garden that Hoichi Kurisu installed, which has transformative effects on patient morale. There was no window in my husband's hospital room where he had been waiting for a medical procedure recently. The nurse switched on the television to show scenes of green pastures. She said this produces a calming effect in anxious patients.

Our gardens protect us from noise and pollution. Vegetation reduces noise pollution through a phenomenon called sound attenuation. Various plants are best because different leaves mitigate different kinds of noises. Plant leaves absorb and deflect sound waves, creating a buffer. They also absorb air pollutants such as ozone, carbon monoxide, and sulfur dioxide.

Horticultural therapy is an ancient practice that is gaining popularity today. The American Horticultural Therapy Association describes it as when a trained therapist uses gardening and plant-based activities to achieve a therapeutic goal. Horticultural therapists utilize a range of gardening activities to treat patients' physical and mental health issues. They have achieved success, for example, with youth who feel alienated, such as some who have committed offenses. The young people report better self-image and confidence after gardening therapy. It is also interesting to note there is an increase in productivity in workplaces with gardens or indoor plants.

CREATING YOUR HEALING GARDEN

Most of us are dealing with some degree of stress in our everyday lives. We would all benefit from a healing garden, bringing nature's positive effects to our physical and mental well-being. Here are eight simple steps for designing a wellness garden at home.

Establish Goals

To help decide which type of healing garden to create, restorative or enabling, list your or your family's three most important health concerns. For example, these are my personal goals:

1. Eat healthy
2. Have less stress
3. Garden as long as possible as I age

This hospital has patient rooms overlooking a healing garden.

There is no more soothing sound than my waterfall.

The fragrance of hostas and other flowers in my Serenity Garden has a calming effect.

A raised bed makes herbs, flowers, or vegetables easier to tend as we age.

I can admire the Serenity Garden from my favorite chair inside the house in all seasons, including winter.

The dawn redwood has many attributes, including the beautiful fall color of its leaves.

To achieve these goals, I created a restorative garden to help reduce stress and an enabling garden that provides fresh vegetables. Adding raised beds makes it easier for me to garden as I age. Your garden should address specific healing needs and accommodate visitors' limitations. Of course, it must also be visually pleasing. Once you decide on your primary goals, it is possible to prioritize design features using elements of the cottage garden style.

Choose a Location

Your healing garden will thrive in sun or shade if you choose plants that will grow in those conditions. I located mine so I can see it from inside the house, meaning I can obtain some of the calming benefits of the healing garden without going outside in inclement weather. The location was initially quite shady due to an ancient silver maple and a diseased catalpa tree. However, they stood in a wet spot that eventually hastened their demise. We replaced them with a dawn redwood, which loves wet feet and is the perfect example of the right plant in the right place.

The healing garden is golden in spring with miniature daffodils. The swing under the arbor invites you to sit. The arbor provides shade.

The ancient cedar tree is an interesting focal point of my Serenity Garden.

The bark of the cedar tree has unique folds and textures.

A tall fence and a vine-covered arbor create a sense of privacy in my healing garden.

The climbing hydrangea is stunning when in bloom.

A Virginia creeper vines its way through the mock hydrangea on the arbor; the vines give shade.

Some shade comes from an old cedar tree. The cedar still lives but has lost its lower branches, leaving a fascinating trunk as a focal point. If you have an attractive tree, rock formation, or other natural element, consider incorporating it into your healing garden.

If your healing garden is in full sun, it will need shade cover, such as an arbor or pergola, giving you a cool place to relax.

Finally, choose a relatively flat spot, especially so someone with mobility issues can enjoy the garden's beauty.

Paths and Fences

Begin with the hardscape, the nonliving elements of the garden, such as paths and fences. Think of the garden as an outdoor room. Use paths and patios to unify the area, connecting it, for example, to the side garden. If you need to accommodate wheelchairs, ensure your paths are wide enough: a 5-foot (1.5 m) minimum is preferred. Path surfaces must be firm and smooth. Consider privacy walls or fences and shade structures. I placed a tall fence with a climbing hydrangea (*Hydrangea anomala*) behind my healing garden. I added an arbor covered with Japanese hydrangea vine (*Schizophragma hydrangeoides*) and Virginia creeper (*Parthenocissus quinquefolia*). The fence and arbor provide privacy. Add some stepping-stones; they are more difficult for wheelchairs, but they encourage the walker to slow down and take time strolling through parts of the garden. They enable you to center yourself. You cannot cross stepping-stones while looking at a cell phone!

Stepping-stones slow visitors as they journey through England's Dorset House cottage garden.

This pretty tiered water fountain is near a rocking chair overlooking the Serenity Garden.

Wooden chimes have a soothing, pensive sound.

If you have space for a pond, you will love its relaxing effects.

The back porch, part of my healing garden, with its wind chime and proximity to a water feature.

Incorporate Water, Sound, and Lighting

A water feature evokes feelings of relaxation. It does not have to be elaborate; a simple rock bubbler will do the trick. I use birdbaths and fountains. A bowl of still water creates reflections and brings more light into the garden. If you have a larger space, consider a pond or waterfall. Studies show that when water features look more natural, they have better therapeutic effects.

The sound of water from a waterfall or fountain encourages contemplation. Or you could hang a wind chime at the entrance to your garden as a veil you go through into your healing space. Hang wooden chimes for their meditative tones in other spots.

If you spend time in your sanctuary in the evening, use LED lighting to set off plants to their best advantage. Drape a string of lights over an arbor or tree. Discreetly placed lights create beautiful shadows and draw attention to colors and textures in your garden.

Attract Wildlife

Create a habitat that encourages wildlife; enjoy its healing energy, such as the enormous mental boost birdsong gives. Attract butterflies, birds, and pollinating insects by providing birdhouses, bird feeders, birdbaths, and the plants they love. Duane tends the birdhouses and feeders in our gardens; he frequently changes the water in birdbaths to keep them clean and suitable for pollinators and bird visitors. Because I am inside the house more often in winter, he places a simple, heated water dish on the Serenity Garden porch so I can watch the birds through the window. I long for that magical time in spring when I can go into the garden to enjoy the morning chorus of birdsong.

Grow plants that supply nectar and food. Joe Pye weed (*Eutrochium purpureum*), tobacco plant (*Nicotiana* spp.), and *Chrysanthemum* 'Sheffield Pink' are nectar-filled favorites; Joe Pye has an exceptionally long nectar-producing period, making it a prime attraction for pollinating insects. Bring in the hummingbirds with a bed of turtlehead. Instead of a commercial hummingbird feeder, I place a hanging basket of fuchsia on the Serenity Garden porch. It has attracted our local ruby-throated hummingbird on a daily basis.

Provide birdhouses to give birds shelter and a place to raise their young.

Ruby-throated hummingbirds visit the fuchsia plant daily.

Wooden chairs near a pond at Chanticleer Gardens in Wayne, Pennsylvania, provide a place to sit and observe the beauty of nature.

A lightweight chair is placed in a favorite spot at Northview.

Provide Seating

Include places to sit and observe the beauty of nature. A simple bench or chair you can move easily to a favorite spot will suffice. Or you may prefer a cozy chair, hammock, or glider.

Take the comfort of your seating area further by transforming it into a secluded retreat defined by sheer curtains or plantings. An outdoor carpet can help define the space. Include an outdoor bookshelf or a blanket box. In the evening, light a few candles or lanterns in your area for added ambiance.

Create Focal Points

Your healing garden should have a focal point for meditation and reflection. Suitable focal points include a piece of sculpture, a unique plant, interesting rocks, or a water fountain. I love statues and have several in my gardens. I also use mirrors as focal points. However, mirrors can confuse birds. Therefore, I don't put mine out until after spring when the birds have finished finding mates. My plants have grown higher by then, hiding much of the mirror from the birds. You can put a sticker on your mirror to deter them. I place mirrors away from birds' flight paths and feeding areas. Position a mirror where it won't cause bright sun reflection or solar heat, which may damage plants. Duane finds mirrors for me in thrift stores; they are an inexpensive and whimsical way to enhance your garden. Placing one in a shady or dappled-light area will brighten the dark space. They add depth and make a small garden appear more spacious.

When adding focal points, be aware that brightly colored objects or other unnatural garden art materials can counter the healing effects of your garden. A few of my focal points follow.

An elegant statue.

*A mirror reflects caladium (*Caladium bicolor*).*

An interesting planter.

A weathered tin birdhouse.

A statue of St. Francis of Assisi.

Choose Plants

When you have finished hardscaping, it's time to choose plants. Reduce maintenance by growing those suited to your climate. Place plants with similar needs (water, sunlight, soil) together. Another tip for lowering maintenance is to use fewer varieties and more of each with the added benefit of providing unity. Remember to plant for abundance in the cottage garden style.

When deciding which plants to add to your healing garden, remember your goals while considering the palette you like. If bright colors energize you, include annuals such as zinnias, sunflowers, petunias, or cosmos. Color stimulates mood and positive emotions. One of my goals was to destress so I used calming blues and greens. Use cheery pink and invigorating red for someone experiencing or recovering from depression; your healing garden should have many purples—purple is similar to blue in the way it makes you feel calm and relaxed. Color psychology, called chromotherapy or color healing, is a new science. There is evidence it helps reduce stress, but more research is needed.

My vision was to accentuate the plants' color, form, and texture in my part-shade garden. I chose textures ranging from bold-leaved hostas to the fern-like foliage and dense, feathery plumes of astilbe (*Astilbe ×arendsii*). An example of diverse shades of color is my choice of chartreuse Japanese forest grass (*Hakonechloa*), and variegated lamium's silver leaves edged with dark green. I love ornamental grasses for the therapeutic garden. They sway in the wind, bringing attention to a soft breeze that may otherwise go unnoticed.

I like to incorporate some plants that touched me as a child. Scent memory is powerful so I grow rosemary, lemon verbena, lavender, and chocolate mint herbs.

Variegated lamium and chartreuse Japanese forest grass in front of a stand of turtlehead blooms add appealing texture and shades of color to my Serenity Garden.

Their therapeutic fragrances take me back to my grandmother's cottage garden and kitchen. Choosing plants that trigger positive emotions from a person's past, such as old-fashioned hollyhocks (*Alcea rosea*) or lilacs (*Syringa vulgaris*), is especially helpful if your healing garden is for someone with Alzheimer's disease.

Avoid thorny and toxic plants. Always choose insect- and disease-resistant varieties to eliminate pesticide use.

Hollyhocks are an old-fashioned flower that may evoke memories and trigger positive emotions.

PLANTS FOR THE HEALING GARDEN

Zinnia (Zinnia elegans)

Turtlehead

Tobacco plant

Chrysanthemum 'Sheffield Pink'

Dahlia

Water lily

Clematis (Clematis *'Tie Dye'*)

Hydrangea (Hydrangea paniculata *'Limelight'*).

Astilbe

HEALING GARDENS FOR INDOOR AND OTHER LIMITED SPACES

If you don't have enough space for the type of healing garden I describe or are not ready to tackle a task of that size, there are options. You may create a healing garden indoors using a variety of houseplants. For limited spaces outdoors create one with pots on a patio, deck, or balcony.

Many people suffer from the winter blues, feeling depressed when the days become shorter. Some have more serious symptoms of severe depression called seasonal affective disorder (SAD), a type of depression related to the change in seasons. SAD occurs in climates with less sunshine at certain times of the year. It is during these three to four months when SAD symptoms are at their worst that sufferers most need the benefits of a healing garden. What are we to do when the garden season is over? I created a winter healing space in my house using houseplants and adding some essential elements of the cottage healing garden.

You won't need a large area for this project. A corner near a window for light with enough room for a few houseplants and a chair will work well. The amount of light and humidity will determine which plants you select, while the size of plants and the space will influence how many you choose. When you buy houseplants, read the light and humidity needs on the plant tag. For example, you will place plants native to tropical jungles, such as snake plants (*Sansevieria* spp.) and philodendrons (*Philodendron* spp.) in low light. Choose desert plants like echeveria and air plants (*Tillandsia*) if your room is hot and dry.

A study in England between RHS Science and the University of Reading analyzed psychological responses

Snake plant

Heartleaf philodendron

Fiddle-leaf fig

Pothos

Rubber plant

to various houseplants. They determined that three plants, pothos (*Epipremnum aureum*), weeping fig (*Ficus benjamina*), and palm (*Dypsis lutescens*), were best for overall well-being. I chose pothos, a fiddle-leaf fig (*Ficus lyrata*), and a rubber plant (*Ficus elastica*) for similar effects to the weeping fig, plus a palm. Pothos likes bright to low, indirect light and weekly watering. Fig plants and rubber plants prefer bright, indirect light or a sunny area with afternoon shade. Palm plants thrive in low light. Avoid overwatering the palm, but keep the soil evenly moist.

Also, consider the easy-to-grow spider plant (*Chlorophytum comosum*). Spider plants like bright light. Water them generously when the soil feels dry. I have had success with a monstera (*Monstera* spp.) plant. It prefers medium light and a deep watering every one

African violet

My indoor healing garden is the perfect remedy for the winter blues.

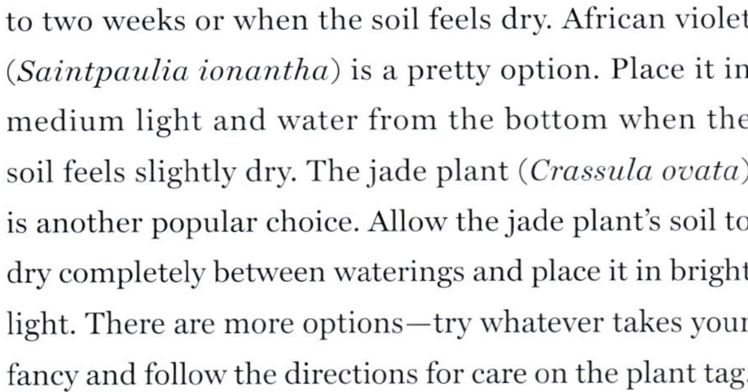

to two weeks or when the soil feels dry. African violet (*Saintpaulia ionantha*) is a pretty option. Place it in medium light and water from the bottom when the soil feels slightly dry. The jade plant (*Crassula ovata*) is another popular choice. Allow the jade plant's soil to dry completely between waterings and place it in bright light. There are more options—try whatever takes your fancy and follow the directions for care on the plant tag.

Put plants at different heights. Consider purchasing a multitiered plant stand if there is little space. Add a water feature—a small tabletop fountain will suffice. A favorite piece of sculpture makes a perfect focal point for meditation and reflection. You will need a comfortable chair; next to it, place a basket with books, magazines, or needlework. Finally, play some relaxing music.

For limited space outdoors, place together a variety of pots of different sizes. Choose plants of varying textures and colors as I describe for the traditional healing garden, considering the amount of sunshine they will receive. Include a rug, a small water feature, and garden art such as a statue. With the addition of a comfortable chair, you can enjoy the healing benefits of the garden in your beautiful small outdoor space. For more ideas, consult my description of sensory gardens for small spaces.

Making a healing garden, indoors or outside, takes time, as does healing and recovering from an illness or traumatic event. Enjoy the journey. As David Culp says, "The strength of the garden is its ability to take you away from the stresses of this world." (Piedmont Landscape Association Conference 2024)

We use our senses to enjoy the buzz of bees and the beauty of flowers, like this pretty anemone (Anemone hupehensis).

The Cottage Garden as a Sensory Garden

Like healing gardens, sensory spaces enhance your well-being, reducing stress as they calm your mind. A sensory garden takes the healing garden a step further; it is like a fine-tuned healing garden. When you walk through a cottage healing garden or any garden, you use your senses to smell the flowers, admire the beautiful blooms you see there, and enjoy the sound of a bee pollinating a border. When you create a cottage garden as a sensory garden, you consciously design it to stimulate and engage the five basic senses of sight, hearing, touch, smell, and taste. You consider the five senses in every aspect, from hardscaping (the nonliving parts of the garden, such as paths and water features) to planting. This type of garden enables you to become more aware of your surroundings and how to respond to them as you connect to nature.

The stimulation provided by a sensory garden is beneficial to both children and adults. Some young friends had a sweet baby girl called Lucy. When they moved into a new house, they had the opportunity to make their first garden together. Lucy's parents wanted her to acquire a knowledge of the natural world. I suggested there is no better way than through a sensory garden. Infants put objects in their mouths, watch their mother's face, and turn toward sounds made by squeaking toys. They learn about their environment through their senses. Lucy has learned from her early experiences in the garden and has grown into a bright little girl who loves plants and gardening.

A sensory garden can offer solace to individuals with varying degrees of exceptionality. For example, for children with autism, the sensory garden can provide a safe place to explore. Adults with mental health issues can benefit from the stimulation the sensory garden provides. Those with visual impairment respond to bold colors and design aspects focusing on touch and sound. Providing colors, textures, and smells will go a long way to reduce the stress caused by hearing loss. A sensory garden can help keep people with dementia calm and interested. For all of us, a sensory garden offers a delightful remedy for today's stressful times.

Lucy loves to choose new plants for her sensory garden.

DESIGN CONSIDERATIONS

Sensory gardens are suitable for small or large spaces. Your design may be for just one sense, such as a fragrance garden, or it may encompass all five senses. The garden should encourage interaction with the environment. Here are some factors to consider.

If your garden is for all five senses, you may either separate your garden into distinct sense zones or mix the five elements to engage multiple senses simultaneously.

Think about the person or persons for whom you are designing the garden and make a list of their needs. Decide how you can meet their requirements. For example, if children will use the space, choose nontoxic plants, and if a wheelchair is necessary, paths must be wide and stable enough. For people with sensory impairments, divide your garden into five clear areas, one sense for each section, so the sensory messages from each are undistorted.

In addition to the plantings, hardscaping elements are crucial. You may include sitting and standing areas with different textures to see and touch. For example,

Tree stump seats and table are a favorite place to rest and enjoy a cool drink in my garden.

In my potting shed, a vintage rocking chair provides comfort, privacy, and protection.

consider grouping a circle of rough-textured tree stumps for seating. Sensory pathways may have various types of surfaces: flagstone, sand, wood chips, or perhaps smooth, flat stepping-stones.

Comfort is essential; therefore, add seating for those who tire easily and provide shelter from the sun. Building or buying a pergola is a lovely option if there are no trees. A shed or hut can be a tranquil setting to relax and enjoy your garden, while at the same time providing privacy and protection from the elements. Create a calm zone with neutral colors that focus on relaxation. Locate your calm spot away from hectic areas. A quiet area is a lovely place for a hammock.

The sensory garden must be a safe place if users are to interact with it. For information or concerns about the toxicity of plants, contact the local Poison Control Center in your area. A directory of these centers is available from The American Association of Poison Control Centers' website. Plants should not only be nontoxic with no pesticide application but also nonallergenic. Blooms pollinated by insects are preferable to plants releasing seeds into the air. Place thorny plants, such as roses, at the back of beds out of reach.

When choosing plants, ensure they will do well in your growing conditions, whether sun or shade, poor or good drainage, clay or another type of soil. Select hardy, durable plants of various heights, colors, textures, and scents for your sensory garden to be interesting as well as beautiful.

THE SENSE OF SIGHT

Contrasting elements of color, form, movement, light, and shadow add to our sensory experience when we look at a beautiful garden. Red, orange, and yellow are warm colors that promote activity. Cool colors such as blue, purple, and white encourage tranquility. To avoid overstimulation, balance energizing colors and restful, soft colors.

Add interesting visual patterns by placing, for example, a red coleus in front of white Shasta daisies. Plant blue delphinium next to a yellow-flowered shrubby cinquefoil. A splash of a single color provides a dramatic effect. Try a swath of bright yellow or orange marigolds; they will be striking, especially in the fall border. Plant some pretty native wildflowers for a calming effect.

Accessories like gazing balls, mirrors, a water feature, and sculptures add to the visual effect. Plant flowers of varying colors and bloom times, foliage of different shapes and sizes, and plants that butterflies love. Some suggestions: bleeding heart (*Lamprocapnos spectabilis*)

Red and yellow are warm colors as this daylily shows.

*An example of cool colors: purple allium (*Allium *'Globemaster'), blue catmint, and white lamb's ear.*

A swath of yellow marigolds is arresting in the fall border.

Plant some pretty native wildflowers for a calming effect.

with flowers that look like downward-facing hearts; blazing star (*Liatris spicata*) with its soft, vertical flower spikes that bloom from the top down; butterfly weed to attract monarch butterflies; Swiss chard 'Bright Lights' exhibiting vibrant, near-fluorescent midribs through the center of the leaves; and tall sunflowers (*Helianthus*) with large, showy blooms that draw butterflies and bees, then later attract birds and squirrels for the seeds.

Swiss chard 'Bright Lights' displays its vibrant leaves that are stunning in a sensory garden.

False sunflower is a golden native flower that pollinators adore.

Although not native to the United States, plants like this pretty, hardy chrysanthemum 'Sheffield Pink' attract pollinators to the fall garden.

A bamboo water feature makes a soothing, trickling sound and a clacking noise that keeps the deer at bay.

THE SENSE OF HEARING

Some sounds in a sensory garden occur without planning—the wind rustling through leaves, for example. I plant native and favorite non-native flowers to attract wildlife such as buzzing bees and other pollinators. Leaving dead leaves on the ground creates a crunching sound underfoot you can enjoy. Plant balloon flowers (*Platycodon grandiflorus*) that will make a popping sound when the buds are squeezed, and ornamental grasses like switchgrass (*Panicum virgatum*) that make a pleasant noise when the wind causes their tall, leafy stems to rub together. My grandchildren loved to shake the seed pods of false indigo (*Baptisia australis*) to hear the seeds rattle.

Enhance the variety of sounds by including dripping or trickling water and wind chimes. Bird feeders and water features encourage our feathered friends to stop by with their sweet songs. Crunchy gravel paths and patios create sounds contrasting with softer elements like moss pathways.

A small patio of white marble chips contrasts with the natural rocks nearby and various plant textures in my sensory garden.

THE SENSE OF TOUCH

When considering touch, think texture. Make a list of textures: rough, smooth, soft, hard, fluffy, and ridged. Write your ideas for each. Include soft flowers, fuzzy leaves, rough bark, prickly seed pods, and springy moss. Place smooth stones in your sensory garden to invite touch. Use them to mark a pathway. Add rough, natural stone boulders as a contrast. Cover the ground with straw or bark mulch to create an area where children and adults can sit, walk, or lie. Structures, like walls and fences, can add a textural element when made of brick or wood. Consider the material you use for seating and decking; for example, soft cushions, chairs with smooth arms, decking with grooves, or cobblestones underfoot. Add a glass, stone, or metal sculpture to personalize the area and provide additional sensory interest. Water or

The touch of Celosia, *with its furry flower heads, contrasts with the rough wood of the window box.*

Lamb's ear at the edge of the border begs you to touch its soft, fuzzy leaves.

sand trickling through the fingers offers a pleasing sensory experience.

The first plant that comes to mind for tactile stimuli is lamb's ear with its soft, fuzzy leaves. I love a similar plant with soft foliage called angel wings (*Senecio candicans*). Yarrow is an excellent example of stiff flowers and soft leaves. Feather reed grass (*Calamagrostis ×acutiflora*), purple coneflower, borage (*Borago officinalis*), Irish moss (*Sagina subulata*), and cockscomb (*Celosia*) are all appealing to touch.

People with visual limitations are aware of how touch is a vital sense for exploring a garden. People without this limitation may underestimate its importance. It may be the most significant of our senses when in the garden as it is how we appreciate the best qualities of the natural world.

THE SENSE OF SMELL

Install a pick-and-sniff bed for herbs or flowers. Think about both subtle and strong smells that can be explored directly (by sticking one's nose in the flower) and indirectly (for example, by stepping on an aromatic groundcover such as creeping thyme). Nasturtium has a delicate aroma, while peony has a heady perfume. Refrain from placing highly fragrant blooms too close together; space them at intervals. Some plants like sweetshrub (*Calycanthus floridus*) and spicebush (*Lindera benzoin*) release their scent when you crush the leaves or petals. The sweetshrub also has interesting seed pods that stimulate the sense of touch.

Include the resinous scent of pine needles and the new smells of fresh mulches and grass clippings. Many herbs have wonderful aromas: rosemary, lemon verbena, lavender, and chocolate mint, for example. Include shrubs like Korean spice viburnum (*Viburnum carlesii*), lilac, and witch hazel (*Hamamelis* spp.). Add perennial catmint, moss phlox, and all lilies. Plant hyacinth bulbs (*Hyacinthus orientalis*) in fall for their sweet, aromatic scent in spring. Scented geraniums (*Pelargonium graveolens*) are another choice; there are several scents available including cedar, lemon, and attar of roses. One of my favorite sensory plants is the chocolate cosmos (*Cosmos atrosanguineus*), which smells like chocolate or vanilla.

Three more plants for the sense of smell are anise hyssop (*Agastache foeniculum*), pineapple sage (*Salvia elegans*), and sweet pea (*Lathyrus odoratus*).

Smells bring back memories. Freshly cut grass, loamy earth, and the sweet fragrance of lupine blooms return me to my mother's garden. You can both evoke the old and make new memories with your beautiful and aromatic sensory garden.

THE SENSE OF TASTE

Everything for tasting must be nontoxic. Grow edible flowers, fresh herbs, vegetables, and fruit, taking care to differentiate them from nonedible plants by placing them together in a designated area.

Here are some suggestions for flowers and their flavors:

- The lavender-pink blooms of chives (*Allium schoenoprasum*) are best harvested when they are just beginning to open. They have a mild onion flavor.
- Try the crisp cucumber flavor of borage.

Nasturtium has a delicate smell and attracts pollinators that stimulate our sense of hearing. It also tastes good.

Crush and sniff sweetshrub flowers for a hint of pineapple and bubblegum.

The sweetshrub plant also has interesting seed pods for touching.

Anise hyssop

Pineapple sage

Sweet pea

- Lavender flowers (*Lavandula angustifolia*) smell wonderful and have a floral taste.
- Bee balm flowers have a citrus, minty taste.
- Violets (*Viola* spp.), Johnny-jump-ups (*Viola tricolor*), and pansies (*Viola ×wittrockiana*) have a sweet, wintergreen or perfumed flavor.

In addition to flowers, consider growing fruits and vegetables. Many fruits, such as strawberries (*Fragaria ×ananassa*) and blueberries (*Vaccinium* spp.) are easy to grow. Edibles usually require cooking before eating, but fruit is ready to nibble right off the plant. My young friend Lucy loves to grow carrots. She enjoys washing them, cooking them with her nana, and eating them. An early introduction to fresh, healthy food helps young children as they begin to make their own food choices.

Herbs such as basil, mint, and parsley are tasty treats. I mentioned lavender and borage flowers—they are herbs. Chamomile is another edible herb. I enjoy making herb teas and serving them in my garden.

SENSORY GARDENS FOR SMALL SPACES

Using containers, you can create a sensory garden in a small space, such as on a balcony or patio. During a recent spring season, my garden experienced several weeks of drought, causing the lawn grass to die over an underground septic tank. At the end of the septic tank area, I had disguised a pipe with a fake rock. The spot looked like a grave with a tombstone. Visitors asked me if I buried one of my horses there as the so-called grave seemed too big for a dog. I had to do something to remove the perception of a burial site in my cottage garden.

Lavender excites two senses: smell and taste.

Grow carrots and other vegetables in your sensory garden.

Lucy loves picking, washing, and eating the carrots she grows.

Cherry tomatoes are perfect for picking and popping into your mouth.

The septic tank without grass looked like a grave site. What could I do?

The site that formerly resembled a grave is now a delightful patio sensory garden with plants in pots for each of the five senses, a comfortable seat, and a water feature.

As it would be impossible to plant in the ground in that spot, I designed a patio with containers for plants. We edged the patio with some of our abundant Pocono Mountain rocks and added a thick layer of crunchy gravel, placing larger stones with the fake one that concealed the pipe. I chose five beautiful containers of different shapes and sizes and arranged them on the new patio. I planted flowers for each sense in the pots: a bright sunflower for sight, angel wings for touch, a strawberry plant for taste, and the herb rosemary for smell. Blue false indigo will provide sound when the seed pods form and are rattled. Meanwhile, the buzzing of bees is perfect for the sense of hearing. I added a comfortable chair with a small table to hold my cup of tea, eventually adding two more pots with tall plants behind the chair to give privacy. A statue of St. Francis and a birdbath completed the arrangement. I love my new sensory garden.

A multisensory technique I learned from a guide when touring a garden in England enables me to tune in to my garden. I take a deep breath and focus on the following:

Five things I can see.

Four things I can touch.

Three things I can hear.

Two things I can smell.

One thing I can taste.

This procedure immediately calms me. Sensory gardens are an innovative way to promote health and nature for everyone; they are the perfect soothing escape.

The bride's bouquet was a very simple arrangement of hydrangea, zinnia, tiny roses, sedum, and yarrow 'The Pearl' from my cutting garden.

The Cottage Garden as a Cutting Garden

During the time of COVID-19, the daughter of a dear friend was to be married. Like many others, the couple canceled their big wedding and opted for a small, intimate one with the reception to be held in my friend's garden. I was honored when the bride asked me to provide the flowers. I was a little nervous, not having done wedding flowers before, but the bride assured me she wanted very simple, casual bouquets for herself and her two little flower girls. She requested that the blooms come from my garden. With the help of my grandson, Jonathan, and several how-to videos we found online, it became an enjoyable and creative project. The wedding party was thrilled with the results. The ceremony was beautiful, the reception was joyous, and the special day greatly lightened the gloom of the pandemic.

It was a September wedding and I was happy to find beautiful blooms at the end of the gardening season. I was thankful for my cutting garden and will show you how I created it. I will explain why you should create a

Each little flower girl carried a posy of small cottage-garden flowers.

We matched the colors of the flower girls' flowers with their dresses.

I am thankful for my cutting garden.

cutting garden, how to construct and care for one, and how to harvest the flowers.

During the pandemic, many worked from home; afterward, some employees continued this trend for at least part of the work week. Working alone led many people to feel anxious and isolated. I found that fresh flowers from the cutting garden on the dining table, kitchen counter, and desk elevated my mood and made me smile—a vital strategy for relieving anxiety.

The cottage garden, with its abundance of colorful blooms, offers many gorgeous arrangements. However, bringing profuse bouquets into the house means a limited show in the garden. You can solve this problem by creating a flower garden specifically for cutting. There are also critical environmental benefits, like reducing the carbon footprint for producing and transporting flowers sold commercially. You can omit your trips to the florist. In addition, you will acquire great satisfaction as you select the seeds and transplants and nurture the beautiful results.

ANNUAL FLOWERS FOR THE CUTTING GARDEN

Annual flowers, an all-star cast of players in your garden, complete their life cycle in a single season but use their time wisely with robust blooms from late spring until fall. Annuals are hard to beat for showy, season-long color. They are lovely for cutting in summer or drying for winter arrangements. Growing them has many advantages: many flower early and continue until the first frost, whereas perennials have a comparatively short bloom time. Annuals are relatively inexpensive and easy

The cottage garden still has a profusion of flowers in autumn. However, creating a separate cutting garden prevents diminishing the cottage garden's fabulous display.

I change the flower arrangements throughout the year.

Spring flowers in the kitchen give me hope for a perfect gardening season.

to grow with the right site and soil preparation. Annuals are temporary, so you can change what you grow every year. They are versatile and come in many sizes and colors. Annuals are great in pots and containers. They allow you to experiment with color, height, texture, and form. Lastly, if you make a mistake, it's for one growing season only—my kind of flower.

When choosing annual plants, the easiest place to start is at the garden center, where you can purchase greenhouse-grown plants that are strong, healthy, simple to transplant, and will bloom earlier than those grown from seed at home. With hundreds of annuals to choose from, some easy ones for your garden include:

Snapdragon (*Antirrhinum majus*)
Begonia (*Begonia* Semperflorens Cultorum Group)
Celosia
Bachelor's button
Cleome (*Cleome hassleriana*)
Coleus (*Coleus scutellarioides*)
Cosmos (*Cosmos bipinnatus*)
Blanket flower (*Gaillardia ×grandiflora*)
Globe amaranth (*Gomphrena globosa*)
Impatiens (*Impatiens*)
Alyssum (*Lobularia maritima*)
Geranium (*Pelargonium*)
Petunia (*Petunia ×atkinsiana*)
Dusty miller (*Senecio cineraria*)
Marigold (*Tagetes erecta*)
Verbena (*Verbena bonariensis*)
Pansy
Zinnia

A pot of annual flowers invites you to enter the kitchen garden.

Zinnia is my favorite annual flower in the cutting garden.

Zinnias and cleome abound in my cutting garden.

Cosmos

Coleus

Globe amaranth

Pansy

More Favorite Annual Flowers for the Cutting Garden.

Choose vigorous-looking, healthy plants with robust root systems. The roots should fill out the pot, but the plant should not be root bound. Match each plant to the light conditions in the site where you will place it. Check the label, and if, for example, it recommends full sun, plant it where it will receive six or more hours of sunlight each day.

Plant most annuals outdoors after the danger of spring frost has passed, in damp soil in the late afternoon on a cloudy day to reduce transplant shock. If your seedlings are in a tray or a flat, remove them by slicing downward through the soil between the plants with a knife. If they are in pots, carefully remove each plant with its soil block intact. Make a hole in the soil and set the plant at the same depth it was growing in the container. Follow the spacing recommendation on the label. Press the soil firmly around the plant before watering (but not so much that the soil becomes compacted).

You can sow the seeds of some plants, such as sunflowers, four o'clocks (*Mirabilis jalapa*), and zinnias,

Snapdragons may also self-seed. We all love free flowers.

Cleome self-seeds generously.

Golden brown-eyed Susans are striking in flower arrangements.

once the soil warms above 60°F (16°C). Follow the instructions on the seed packet. Some seeds require special care to aid germination; for example, soak morning glory seeds in warm water and scratch nasturtium seeds with a nail file before planting. Your seeds may find the soil in your garden less appealing than the seed-starting mix. They may fail to germinate if the soil cakes and prevents water from entering. To avoid these problems, make furrows or holes, plant the seeds to the depth prescribed on the seed packet, and cover them with moist vermiculite. It is essential to keep the soil moist. When the seeds sprout, thin them to the required spacing. Many annuals, such as cleome and snapdragons, will self-seed, giving you free flowers, but not necessarily where you want them. Thin them if you keep them, or hoe them out like weeds.

THINK BEYOND ANNUALS

We tend to associate cutting gardens with annuals, but you should also consider perennials and woody plants. You need flower varieties with long, sturdy stems and blooms that last a long time in a vase. I also like to include fragrant blossoms in my bouquets because the scent is often missing from store-bought flowers. When buying from a plant catalog or purchasing seeds, you can find varieties best suited for cutting by looking for the scissors icon in the description or on the packet.

The College of Agricultural Sciences conducts trials to identify the best flowers for cutting at the Penn State research farm in Landisville. Here are some of my favorites from their list: black-eyed Susan (*Rudbeckia hirta* 'Indian Summer'), calendula (*Calendula officinalis* 'Indian Prince'), celosia (*Celosia* 'Cramer's Amazon'),

Roses are my favorite woody plant for bouquets. They add scent as well as beauty.

cosmos (*Cosmos* Versailles Mix), dahlia (*Dahlia* Karma® Series), Shasta daisy (*Leucanthemum ×superbum* 'Marconi'), snapdragon (*Antirrhinum majus* Rocket Mix), yarrow (*Achillea millefolium* 'Summer Pastels'), and zinnia (*Zinnia elegans* Benary's Giant Mix).

Other favorites of mine include globe amaranth (*Gomphrena globosa* 'QIS Purple'), lady's mantle (*Alchemilla mollis*), larkspur (*Delphinium* Pacific Giant Mix), purple coneflower (*Echinacea purpurea* 'Magnus'), sweet pea, and sunflower (*Helianthus annuus* 'Double Quick Orange').

Woody plants suitable for cutting are forsythia (*Forsythia* spp.), lilac (*Syringa vulgaris* 'Sensation'), Pinky Winky® hydrangea (*Hydrangea paniculata* 'DVP Pinky'), and roses (*Rosa* spp.).

Your choices should continue into fall with bloomers such as blue spirea (*Caryopteris ×clandonensis* 'Sapphire Surf'™), goldenrod (*Solidago rugosa* 'Fireworks'), and hardy garden chrysanthemum 'Sheffield Pink'. I believe, however, that the best fall flower for vases is the dahlia listed previously.

Dahlias, with their beautiful colors and exquisite forms, make the most stunning fall arrangements.

Yarrow

Shasta daisy

MORE FAVORITE COTTAGE GARDEN PERENNIALS FOR CUTTING

Chrysanthemum 'Sheffield Pink'

Echinacea

Helianthus

Phlox 'David'

Hydrangeas are lovely in flower arrangements. This is 'Pinky Winky'.

PREPARING THE SITE

If you lack space, grow your cutting garden in pots. Use annuals in containers because you can pack them together better than most perennials. Otherwise, pick a sunny, well-drained site and work in plenty of compost. My cutting garden is part of my vegetable garden, but you can locate it in any sunny corner of your yard. Every other year, test your soil fertility with a soil test kit from your local Extension office. Use the results you receive from the university report to add the recommended amendments. Your flowers will last longer when cut if they have proper soil nutrition.

PLANTING YOUR CUTTING GARDEN

Like a vegetable garden, the purpose of a cutting garden is productivity, so plant the flowers in widely spaced rows to allow for easy maintenance. You need not be concerned with color combinations or how the plants look together. It is a good idea to plant flowers with similar sun, water, and drainage requirements together, though. Do not place taller plants where they will shade out shorter ones.

CARING FOR YOUR FLOWERS

Apply organic mulch, such as mushroom compost or leaf mold, to help retain moisture and smother weeds. Organic material improves the soil when it breaks down. Most plants need 1 inch (2.5 cm) of water each week. It is better to use a soaker hose than a handheld watering wand for the water to penetrate at least 6 to 8 inches (15.2 to 20.3 cm) into the soil. A soaker hose applies the water slowly and directly to the roots with less runoff and evaporation. Some plants, for example, zinnias and bee balm, are prone to powdery mildew. This fungus is

I plant my seedlings in an easy-to-manage raised bed.

Correct watering will keep your zinnias and bee balm healthy.

The entrance to the Chelsea Flower Show is always stunning. The show gave its name to the Chelsea Chop.

less likely to occur when you don't wet the leaves while watering.

Pinching is the process of removing the tips of the plant, the small developing leaves at the end of the stems, to make the plant bushier and shorter. For example, petunia, snapdragon, verbena, and zinnia respond well to pinching. I like to give some of my plants the Chelsea Chop, a pruning method that limits the size and often decreases the flopping of several tall herbaceous perennials so you don't need to stake them. It got its name from the Chelsea Flower Show, which takes place in late May in England. The best time to use this pruning method is late spring or early summer, or when the plant has a relatively substantial amount of vegetative growth. Using sharp, clean hand pruners, cut back the stems by making a sloping cut just above a leaf joint. I cut back the plants by a third except for leggy plants that I cut back by a half.

With the Chelsea Chop, flowers will be more numerous and the plant will be bushier. You can do it only on some perennial and annual flowers, but not on woody plants. I perform the Chelsea Chop on black-eyed Susan, coneflower, goldenrod, phlox, and Shasta daisy. Also, I find zinnias benefit from cutting back. I don't do it, however, if we have had a very dry spring that causes the plants to be stressed—I don't want to stress them further.

Deadheading removes flowers once they begin to fade to prevent the formation of seeds. Seed creation slows flower production. If you want to avoid self-seeding, deadhead your flowers faithfully. Not only does deadheading ensure neatness, but it also keeps many plants flowering longer and more profusely.

If the younger leaves become yellow, your plants may be lacking nitrogen. Apply a side dressing of granular fertilizer or a liquid fertilizer such as fish emulsion. Fertilize at peak flowering times; I use a diluted liquid seaweed solution. Cut the flowers frequently to encourage the plant to keep producing blooms. When your annual plants stop flowering, pull them out, lightly cultivate the bed, and replant. For example, replace dying spring flowers such as snapdragons and dianthus with summer bloomers. I treat tulip bulbs as annuals because they rarely bloom a second year in my garden. Therefore, I pull them out when they finish blooming and purchase new bulbs the next year. If you keep them, do not cut them back until the leaves have died or you will have no blooms next spring; the leaves need to absorb the sun to feed the bulbs for next year's flowers. After removing dead leaves, you may plant over the bulbs.

I replace spring tulips with annual summer flowers when they finish blooming.

Use fresh water and recut the stems underwater so your arrangement will last longer.

HARVESTING AND ARRANGING THE FLOWERS

The best time to harvest is early morning when the dew has dried and before the day's heat. Harvest each flower when its buds are just starting to open or have recently opened, and put the cut stems in tepid water immediately. Strip off the leaves and thorns because, when submerged, the plant tissue will decay and shorten the life of your arrangement.

Put clean water in the vase. The flowers will last longer in acidic water, which is achieved by using a floral preservative. Follow the directions indicating the ratio of water to preservative. Don't add extra water, which will reduce the effectiveness of the floral preservative. An overdiluted floral preservative solution has enough sugars to feed the bacteria, but it does not contain enough bactericide to control them, resulting in a shorter vase life for the flowers.

Before placing each stem in the vase, cut it to expose fresh tissue that will better take up water. Cut off about ½ inch (1.2 cm) underwater in a bowl in the sink, and immediately place the stem in the vase. Check the water level daily. Recut stems and replace the water every few days.

Yarrow 'The Pearl' is a perennial that makes a long-lasting filler for flower arranging.

The bold blossoms of a giant marigold make a statement in an arrangement.

When arranging flowers, a bouquet should be about three times as tall as its vase. Select three types of flowers for your arrangement: bold blossoms (dahlias, giant marigolds, hydrangeas, peonies, roses, sunflowers, or zinnias) to make a statement; spiky blooms (delphinium, foxglove, or salvia) to add height and drama; and airy flowers (catmint, lady's mantle, or even the flowers or seedheads of dill) for filling. My favorite flower for filling is yarrow, 'The Pearl'. I often break the rules as my flower arrangements are straightforward and casual, reflecting the style of my cottage garden.

Indulge yourself with ever-changing combinations of flowers inside your home. You will find that even small arrangements not only add beauty to your surroundings but also bring a touch of nature indoors and provide you with months of enjoyment.

Provide child-size tools and equipment.

CHAPTER 7

Leave a Legacy

Children must be allowed time in their early years to interact with nature and living elements before they can understand it well enough to want to preserve it.

—VICKI STOECKLIN

I want my legacy to be a garden where I have made a difference by improving the environment, with my descendants continuing the work. Every gardener can play an essential part in solving today's global problems, but it will take more than one generation to complete the task. The children in our lives (they don't have to be our own) are our hope for the future. This final chapter provides tools to instill a love for gardening in children. I begin with hints for teaching children the fundamentals of gardening, then share how I made a child's cottage garden, and conclude with year-round activities to keep children's interest at a peak.

Gardening with Children

I'll never forget the look of joy on my grandson Jonathan's face when he saw the first sprout of a seed he'd planted or the pride his brother, Harry, displayed when he finished creating his very own garden with just one tomato and two pepper plants. As I witnessed my grandchildren's delight, I had hope because gardening was teaching them a sense of responsibility, which is the first step to becoming stewards of the earth. I find gardening with children genuinely magical.

THE BENEFITS OF GARDENING WITH CHILDREN

What better way for children to indulge a love of digging in the dirt than through gardening? There are many benefits: Allowing them the opportunity to nurture a plant generates a love of nature while also fostering learning. Children develop science and math skills as they predict, measure, and care for the plant's ongoing growth. They learn botany, ecology, environmental science, and zoology through gardening experiences, often more effectively than in the classroom. Since they are active learners, children learn best when the emphasis is on interaction, play, and discovery—the type of activities gardening provides.

Keeping a garden journal improves writing and drawing abilities. Children acquire social skills by working with other children and adults while cherishing this special time spent with you. Planting an extra row reinforces the importance of generosity as they share what they grow. They expand life skills such as responsibility, independence, and problem-solving.

There are physical and mental benefits for children when digging, moving the soil, pushing a wheelbarrow, and carrying a heavy watering can. Through these activities, children develop gross motor skills and overall strength. According to a 2024 article, "Gardening with Kids: How It Affects Your Child's Brain, Body, and Soul," published by the Public Broadcasting Service, heavy physical activities have been shown to help children stay calm and focused. The hard work improves mood and decreases anxiety. The medical doctors who wrote the article also discuss the theory that a lack of childhood exposure to germs increases a child's likelihood of acquiring diseases such as asthma. In addition, the development of the child's immune system becomes suppressed, leading to allergies and autoimmune conditions.

Gardening teaches patience as children learn that immediate results are not part of the gardening experience. Acquiring that life lesson will not only help them more fully enjoy planting and nurturing the garden, but will also serve them well in many circumstances. As an added benefit, children are much more likely to eat what they grow, fostering healthy eating habits.

DEVELOPMENTALLY APPROPRIATE GARDENING ACTIVITIES

You must include the child in making decisions as you garden together. Consider the child's age and give age-appropriate choices; for example, two options are enough for children under five. Very young children may need and enjoy a play garden where they can dig, water, plant, and replant. In the play garden, provide containers with rocks (not too small as they may go into

Grandson Jonathan loves eating vegetables, perhaps because he has helped in my garden since he was very young.

Finding an interesting insect is a teachable moment.

mouths), bark, and garden-related items for the child to explore; add some earth-mover toys, too. You can help children aged five to eight grow various full-size plants, but even with older children, forget adult ideas about gardening. While you may require straight rows of vegetables in your perfect garden, the children may have other plans. Look for the teachable moment: You planned to pull weeds, but the children found an interesting bug; this is a perfect opportunity to explore and learn together.

Children have preferred learning styles, which may be visual, auditory, or tactile. Provide a variety of activities to allow the children to use their preferred modes and develop those areas where they may need to be stronger. The child who is a visual learner may enjoy drawing a garden plan or watching you demonstrate how to plant a flower; the auditory learner may get to know the names of plants by listening to you talk about them; and the tactile learner will need to touch flower petals and get their hands in the dirt.

The garden changes constantly, providing a hands-on approach to learning. Importantly, though, gardening is fun!

PLANNING: GET READY TO DIG

Involve the child in the planning. Explain that plants, like us, need food and drink and that a healthy garden needs good soil. Together, choose a spot that receives enough sun and is near a water source. Locate the garden where others can admire it. You can use carpet squares for pathways to clearly define the places to walk, avoiding frequent warnings not to step on the plants. If you have very little space, let your child choose containers of different sizes in which to plant their garden.

Keep this first garden small so it will be manageable. Consider converting your child's old sandbox to a garden bed. The child will be comfortable working in a familiar space. You may need to relocate it, however, for optimum growing conditions. Modular raised beds are suitable for a child's garden and are readily available.

Plan to add whimsy, such as garden ornaments that the child picks out from a store or catalog. Fairy lights create a sense of wonder. Incorporate living structures, like bean teepees, to create hidden nooks and hiding places. Elements like these encourage outdoor play and foster creativity.

Include birdhouses and native plants to encourage wildlife into the garden. Have the child select a spot for a chair where they can relax and observe the comings and goings of insect and bird visitors. Older children can keep a nature journal, noting how wildlife changes throughout the year.

TOOLS FOR CHILDREN

Children should have their own garden tools. Those for planting and digging should be child-size but sturdy. For little children, old, heavy kitchen spoons work well for digging and measuring cups for scooping. Older children may use regular trowels and cultivators, especially plastic ones, as these are lighter and safer, but avoid cheap, flimsy plastic tools that break easily.

A child-size watering can helps. Provide buckets, plastic pots, and perhaps a wheelbarrow that match the child's size for moving rocks and compost. It is important to give them work gloves that fit.

A small, modular raised bed is perfect for a child's garden.

Encourage the child to pick a whimsical item for the garden.

Incorporate a living structure, such as a bean teepee.

Children love the spiky texture of hens and chicks—and they love the little chicks.

SAFETY IN THE GARDEN

Supervise all activities and materials when working with young children. Teach them how to handle garden tools safely. Explain they should wear shoes when using tools to avoid cuts and bruises on their feet. Do not use animal manure in the garden because it may harbor harmful microorganisms. Avoid commercial pesticides, even those labeled "organic," as children are especially vulnerable to their effects, and we know children love to touch things, then put their fingers in their mouth. Bear in mind that some seeds and bulbs may have a harmful chemical coating. Do not use seeds with children under the age of three. Research and reject poisonous plants before a problem arises. If in doubt about a plant's toxicity, call or email the local Extension office. Teach children not to touch or ingest any plants without your permission.

PLANTS TO PICK

Start with easy-to-grow, disease-resistant and pest-resistant plant varieties. Remember that the child, with adult guidance, should be involved in deciding which plants to purchase. Next, choose plants that appeal to sight, touch, and smell. Try sturdy ones such as pole beans and sunflowers. Grow sensory plants like fuzzy lamb's ear, prickly squash vines, rubbery begonias, and smooth peppers. Grow plants of different sizes, such as tall sunflowers, huge-leaved squashes, and tiny-leaved thyme. Easy-to-grow plants include basil, marigolds, peppers, tomatoes, and zinnias. Hens and chicks, a hardy succulent, doesn't require much water. Children love the plant's offsets, or chicks, that look like miniatures of the mother plant.

Try miniature super-sweet tomatoes such as 'Sun Gold' or 'Yellow Pear', a cherry tomato that produces

When these cherry tomatoes ripen, they are suitable for popping in your mouth right off the vine.

abundant sweet, bite-size yellow fruit. When very young, my grandson loved to pop cherry tomatoes in his mouth right off the vine. Sow pumpkins and gourds; their large seeds germinate quickly. Children love to choose seed packets and starter plants for their gardens. After planting, remember to put the empty seed packet or plastic marker in the soil next to the plant.

TIPS FOR GARDENING WITH CHILDREN

Involve the child in the whole process—from planting to harvesting. They will learn that gardening is more than play and contributes to the family's well-being. Visit the garden daily to monitor for plant problems, teach them to identify issues, and together make a list of tasks that need to be done. Make caring for the garden fun: Create a wheel with a spinner and have adults and children take turns spinning the dial to see who does each job. Another option is to write tasks on individual index cards—each adult and child picks a card to see the assigned task. Place a garden calendar in your child's room or on the refrigerator. The child crosses off the days after completing each task.

Emphasize fun and creativity: Encourage child-created art, water elements, journaling, and cooking of the harvested produce. Send photographs of the child's garden to family and friends near and far. Invite family and friends to a gathering to celebrate your children's accomplishments and enjoy the food they produce.

When you garden with children, not only will the plants grow, but your children will also grow in many delightful ways.

Creating a Child's Cottage Garden

My young friend Lucy was elated when I suggested we make her own cottage garden at her grandmother Janet's house in Charlottesville, Virginia. She was doubly excited with my suggestion to include a miniature fairy garden in the design. That same day, while shopping for miniature fairies and other supplies, Lucy told the clerk and a few customers that she was making an English cottage garden. On the way to the park, she also informed the nice man down the street who was out spreading mulch. She couldn't contain her excitement.

I was excited, too, especially as Janet gave us carte blanche to dig up her yard. As I had gardened with Lucy two years before, when she was only three years old, I knew how much she loved choosing, planting, and caring for her flowers. Lucy has taken the first steps, strides really, toward stewardship of our earth.

I gardened with Lucy when she was three years old. She is an accomplished little gardener.

DESIGNING THE GARDEN

Here is a simple, step-by-step procedure for designing a child's cottage garden:

1. Include the child in making decisions about their garden. This is essential. Before starting the design, I asked Lucy what colors she would like for the flowers. She picked pink, purple, blue, and red. I suggested she incorporate yellow because she loves sunflowers, and I could include a shorter variety of perennial helianthus. She agreed, and we achieved the first cottage garden element—a riot of color.
2. Together, pick a suitable spot for the garden. We located Lucy's garden at the front of her grandmother's house so people passing by could admire its beauty. We would eliminate some of the lawn area, achieving the goal of less lawn grass. The space receives sun for more than six hours daily, which is excellent exposure for cottage garden plants.
3. Obtain a soil test from the local Extension office before preparing the flower bed. The results will inform you of any necessary amendments.
4. Make a simple sketch. Keeping the garden small, draw its shape on graph paper with an arrow pointing north. If you prefer, a simple hand-drawn sketch will suffice as long as the measurements are clearly labeled. I made Lucy's garden an oval shape 12 by 8 feet (3.7 by 2.4 m) on the axis lines. I added a path 1½ feet (45.7 cm) wide,

Lucy chose a mermaid statue for her cottage garden.

winding through the garden and ending at a spot where we would put the miniature fairy garden. The beds on either side of the path were 2 to 3 feet (61 to 91 cm) wide. The flower beds' gentle curves (inside the oval) are another element of an English cottage garden. Of course, a path isn't mandatory, but be sure the beds are not too wide for the child to get around and tend them.

5. Add a water feature and focal points. Lucy chose a birdbath for her garden that satisfied both elements.
6. Draw in a vertical element. I added a trellis for a vine. Lucy's grandmother chose an obelisk that was even more suitable for the space. If you make the garden against a wall or fence, vertical elements are simple to add.
7. Consider whimsical items; I tasked Lucy with choosing them. She found a concrete mermaid statue, two fairies, and other miniature garden items for the fairy garden.

PREPARING THE SPACE

Here are the supplies you will need:

- Edging material, such as landscaping bricks for outside the entire garden
- Mushroom compost
- Amendments recommended based on the soil test results
- Trellis, water feature, and whimsical items
- Mulch, such as shredded cedar mulch

If you are making a path, you will also need:

- Landscape fabric and staples; not environmentally friendly so you may prefer a layer of sand, but I find the gravel material disappears into the soil without the fabric
- Edging trim to keep the path material in place
- Pea gravel (⅜ inch, or 0.95 cm) or other material such as wood chips

The equation to calculate how much mushroom compost, gravel, or wood chips you need is length × width × height, giving you the amount in cubic units.

Procedure for Preparing the Garden

1. Mark the bed with landscape chalk. Remove the grass. We edged our bed with landscape edging bricks.
2. Mark the path and edge it.
3. Lay landscape fabric along the length of the path, holding it in place with landscape staples. The fabric will separate the soil from the path material.
4. Cover the fabric with gravel or wood chips to a depth of 2 to 3 inches (5 to 7.6 cm); any less will encourage annual weeds. Janet chose gravel. Smooth the gravel path with the flat side of a rake, making it slightly higher in the middle to prevent rain from puddling.
5. Amend the soil, if necessary, with about 3 inches (7.6 cm) of mushroom compost. (Janet's soil contains a lot of clay. The compost will loosen the clay and make it drain better.) You are now ready to plant.

Mark the bed and remove the grass.

Janet followed my drawing exactly and, with some help, she prepared Lucy's garden before we arrived. We just needed to add compost and more gravel before heading to the garden center to choose plants. Oh, and we had to make the fairy garden. Lucy was thrilled when she saw that my grandson, Jonathan, traveled to Charlottesville with us to help her make it. Jonathan has made several miniature gardens for me; I consider him an expert at this task.

CHOOSING THE PLANTS

Because this is a garden for a child, some traditional cottage garden plants are unsuitable: Foxgloves and delphinium are poisonous and roses have thorns. Contact your local Extension office for nontoxic plants suitable for your location. I worked with a master gardener from the Piedmont office in Charlottesville, Virginia, because the zone and conditions at Janet's house are very different from my garden in the Poconos. I produced a list based on Lucy's color preferences and the decision to use as many native plants as possible. Choosing plants of different heights and textures is also a good idea. Here are the plants we chose with the required number following:

- Threadleaf coreopsis (*Coreopsis verticillata* 'Moonbeam'), 1
- Geranium (*Geranium ×johnsonii* 'Johnson's Blue'), 3
- Narrow-leaved sunflower (*Helianthus salicifolius* 'Low Down'), 3
- Blazing Star, gayfeather (*Liatris spicata* 'Kobold'), 3
- Coral honeysuckle (*Lonicera sempervirens*), 1
- Garden phlox (*Phlox paniculata* 'David'), 2
- Garden phlox (*Phlox paniculata* 'Jeana'), 2
- Moss phlox 'Purple Beauty', 5
- Black-eyed Susan (*Rudbeckia hirta* 'Autumn Colors'), 3
- Stonecrop (*Sedum ternatum*), 5
- Spiderwort (*Tradescantia virginiana*), 1
- Zinnias I grew from seed

Lucy chose a very healthy hardy geranium. She selected a pink one, as they didn't have the 'Johnson's Blue' on our list.

Choosing plants at the garden center is enormous fun with Lucy, who takes the task seriously, giving each plant careful consideration. Be prepared to not be able to find all of the plants you want at the garden center. If this is the case, look for similar substitutes or visit more than one plant shop. Allow the child to pick out substitutes they like. Remember to buy only healthy-looking plants.

If some plants on your list are not yet blooming at the garden center, show the child the picture on the plant's tag so they can make an informed choice.

Lucy placed five moss phlox on her cart.

I told Lucy to look at the picture on the plant's tag because the plant was not yet blooming.

Lucy helped load the car with all our wonderful purchases.

PLANTING

Back at the child's garden, place each plant in the spot shown on your sketch, moving them around until you achieve the desired effect. With cottage garden design, you may place them closer than the label specifies to obtain a look of fullness. Be aware, however, that this means you may need to separate the plants more often over the years.

If the child is old enough, this is the perfect opportunity to demonstrate the correct planting procedure. Show them how to dig a hole as deep as the pot and twice as wide. Carefully remove the plant from the container. It is important to tease the roots out of the root ball to loosen them. This is Lucy's favorite gardening activity; she enjoys making teasing noises. I remind her it is okay to tease a plant but may be unkind to tease a person. Place the plant in the hole, spreading out the roots. Instruct the child to backfill the hole with the soil you removed and gently press the soil down. The garden soil should be the same level as in the pot.

When you have planted all the flowers, water them well and add a light layer of mulch, not too deep or it may stop the plants from spreading and creating the effect of fullness typical of a cottage garden. Lucy enjoyed pouring water into the birdbath—her garden was nearly finished. We chose finely shredded cedar mulch as the finishing touch for her beautiful new cottage garden.

ADDING WHIMSY

Young children may want to fill their gardens with garish-looking garden ornaments. To avoid the effect of clutter, unless you don't mind it, suggest they rotate the ornaments, choosing just two or three to display at one time.

We placed each plant in the spot shown on our sketch.

Lucy remembered the correct planting procedure from her previous gardening experiences.

Spiderwort, threadleaf coreopsis, with three hardy geraniums, and garden phlox along the path leading to the miniature garden.

Lucy added water to the birdbath.

We added finely shredded cedar mulch as the finishing touch.

With the help of my grandson, Jonathan, Lucy made a whimsical fairy garden for her cottage garden (see Create a Fairy Garden, page 227). Where did this charming gardening practice come from? Fairy gardens date back to Victorian times with the popularity of the Japanese practice of bonsai and miniature trees. In England, in the mid-1900s, a British nursery owner named Anne Ashberry created small gardens that could be taken care of easily by people who lived in small spaces or by individuals with physical impairments. I like making miniature gardens with children and adults new to gardening because they can learn a lot of sound garden practices from them, such as garden design, choosing appropriate flowers, and caring for plants. They allow you to use your imagination and bring fun to the garden. As whimsy is an element of a cottage garden, fairy gardens are well suited to them. They personalize the garden with their uniqueness. In some cases, they can evoke memories. Jonathan made one in a tin bathtub that was Duane's as a baby. Of course, the grandchildren could not believe their Pappy could fit inside it—even as an infant.

Jonathan made a miniature garden for my cottage garden.

A stumpery inhabited by tiny gnomes in my garden.

Lucy and Jonathan celebrated the completion of the cottage garden with an English tea party.

Gnomes, another beloved garden ornament, infuse the space with whimsy. My mother held a special fondness for them. If you're drawn to them for your garden, you'll find a plethora of options in the gardening sections of various stores, or online. Jonathan once fashioned a stumpery, a gnome-inhabited sanctuary, in my garden, evoking fond memories of my mother's love for these whimsical creatures.

CELEBRATING YOUR CHILD'S ACHIEVEMENTS

An English tea party is the perfect way to celebrate the completion of an English cottage garden. The child could invite some young friends or keep it a family affair. Tiny cucumber sandwiches, scones or cupcakes, and apple juice (tea for the adults) are suitable refreshments. A teapot with cups and saucers add to the atmosphere. Hold the party outside, if possible, allowing the child to explain to partygoers how she made her beautiful cottage garden.

Lucy's pride in her achievements is evident. She will take valuable memories like these into adulthood, becoming a lifelong gardener aware of the importance of preserving our precious environment.

In just a few weeks, the garden bloomed with Lucy's excellent care.

Continued Learning in the Cottage Garden

As a young girl, I wandered the nearby Hednesford Hills in England and picked flowers in the meadows, alone or with friends, confident no harm would come to me. We played in each other's gardens without feeling fearful. Today's children may not have the luxury of a similar carefree existence. For example, they may hear adults discussing problems such as unpredictable weather events and other environmental concerns. Seemingly, every day, the news media reports another climate disaster. As a result, children and adults may experience the type of fear that Yale University experts call climate anxiety, also referred to as eco-anxiety, eco-grief, or climate doom. Our goal is to instill in the next generation a commitment to saving their piece of earth through a love of gardening. We can achieve this goal without the child feeling anxious or afraid.

We want children to grow up to be environmentally aware and proactive without experiencing anxiety. Therefore, we need to tell them what people and communities are doing and demonstrate what they can do now to address the climate issue. Take them to a local community garden where they can see the joyous work of volunteers. If you live in a city such as Philadelphia, visit a neighborhood park like Love and Peace Park in Norris Square, which is part of Las Parcelas and covers more than twenty city lots. Help children understand that urban gardens offer a green respite for residents who want to grow food and find community.

Several colleges, such as Cornell University, have developed programs for children and youth to teach conservation concepts. Cornell's comprehensive project, Gardening in Our Warming World: Youth Grow!, is

I am committed to saving my piece of earth through a love of gardening and strive to instill this in my children and grandchildren.

Love and Peace Park in Norris Square, Philadelphia, is a beautiful example of an urban community garden where volunteers are making a difference.

Demonstrate a love of gardening and gaining pleasure from hard work.

for grades three through twelve. The curriculum offers self-reflective and inspiring activities exploring the positive actions of people and communities. They use a less alarming tone to prevent climate anxiety. Children need to know there is something they can do about today's environmental problems; this knowledge will lessen their feelings of helplessness.

Doug Tallamy is one of the founders of the Homegrown National Park, a grassroots endeavor motivating homeowners and others to plant native plants. Tallamy says, "Don't think about the entire planet's problems—you'll get depressed—instead, focus on the piece of the earth you can influence." Wise words for adults and children alike.

Caring for a cottage garden provides numerous enjoyable, child-friendly activities that show children there is something positive they can do to promote a healthy environment. We should encourage children and youth to unplug, get outside, and dig! They will learn about sustainable gardening including composting, recycling, wise use of water, and gardening without pesticides and herbicides. It is vital to persuade the child without using pressure. Coercion can put them off gardening for life. Demonstrate your love for gardening tasks, setting the example of gaining pleasure from hard work.

Year-round ventures keep the children's interest in gardening and nature alive as you let them know they are making a difference. The following are gardening activities I have tried and tested with children. I describe some outdoor projects for pleasant spring, summer, and fall days and ten garden-related indoor activities for inclement weather or cold winter months.

SUMMER ACTIVITIES

Here are five fun outdoor activities for spring and summertime.

Plant a Beanpole Teepee or a Sunflower House

A beanpole teepee or sunflower house will provide children with their own private space in the garden.

- MATERIALS FOR A TEEPEE: Four to six bamboo poles, strong string or twine, pole bean seeds.
- METHOD: Place the bamboo poles side by side on the ground. Tie them together at the top with string. Stand the poles upright and pull out the legs. Plant any type of pole bean at the base of each pole.
- MATERIALS FOR A SUNFLOWER HOUSE: A packet of sunflower seeds, string, a piece of carpet, or thyme seeds.
- METHOD: Plant sunflowers in a circle or square, leaving a space for entry. When the flowers have grown and are flowering, tie the tops together loosely near the heads to make a hideout.

Cover the floor with a section of old carpet or plant some thyme as a scented groundcover that the child can step upon.

Make a Pizza Garden

Instead of planting in a square or rectangle, children may enjoy a pizza garden planted in a circle and divided into wedge-shaped sections.

- MATERIALS: Landscape chalk and plants such as basil, garlic, onions, peppers, and tomatoes.
- METHOD: Mark the pizza shape and wedges with landscape chalk. Help the child plant a different pizza ingredient in each section. If there is more than one child, assign each section to a different child to plant the ingredients they choose.

Design a Rainbow Garden

Planting a rainbow garden is a great way to teach a child colors.

- MATERIALS: Plants that represent the colors of the rainbow: red salvia, orange marigolds, yellow marigolds, green parsley, dark blue petunias, purple verbena, and pink/lavender ageratum.
- METHOD: The adult and child may plant them randomly or they may plant them in an arch formation to replicate the shape of a rainbow.

Red columbine

Blue cornflower and yellow coreopsis

Orange marigold

Green hens and chicks

Purple lavender

MORE PLANTS FOR A RAINBOW GARDEN

Pink zinnia

Let your child choose a variety of flowers to press.

Press Flowers

Flower pressing became very popular in Victorian England. It was one of my favorite childhood occupations. The Japanese made pictures with pressed flowers, an occupation called oshibana, dating back to the sixteenth century. It is an enjoyable way for children to learn the names of flowers.

MATERIALS: Small cottage garden flowers, scissors, an old book, heavy books to make a press, a sheet of paper and some cardstock for pressing the flowers, a sheet of paper or card for displaying the pressed flowers, tweezers, glue, small paintbrush, and a picture frame.

METHOD: Let the child choose flowers to press from the cottage garden. Explain that small flowers like pansies and daisies are best because bigger plants take longer to dry. Have the child include the stalk when picking the flowers. You may need to help with scissors or snippers.

Have the child arrange the flowers on a piece of paper inside an old book. Place a piece of cardstock on top, close the book, and pile it with several more books as heavy as possible to create a press. Place the press near a sunny window. Every few days, ask the child to check to see if the flowers are dry. If the stem makes a mark when pressed with a fingernail, it needs more time, which takes about two weeks.

When dry, use tweezers to remove the flowers from the book press and arrange them on a sheet or card. Glue them in place carefully, applying the glue to the back of each flower with a small paintbrush. Encourage the child to add the name of each flower and the date it was collected. Mount or frame the pressed flower sheet to display in the child's room.

A sweet little fairy makes a miniature garden delightful.

Create a Fairy Garden

My grandson, Jonathan, made his first miniature garden when he was seven. He has made several more for me over the years and helped Lucy create one for her cottage garden.

MATERIALS: A container with holes, weed block fabric, small rocks, potting mix, and miniature items such as miniature fairies and miniature plants.

METHOD:

1. Put weed block fabric over the holes in the container, add a few inches of rocks, and fill the container with potting mix.
2. Add miniature items such as houses, bridges, garden furniture, and people. These items will add charm to the child's creation.
3. Plant miniature plants. In shady areas, miniature hostas work well. Hens and chicks are appropriate for sunny areas. I have seen a few tiny chicks arranged in rows to make a garden of cabbages. Children love jade plant (*Crassula ovata* 'Ogre's Ears').
4. Instruct the child to water the new plants in the delightful miniature garden.

LUCY'S FAIRY GARDEN

After covering the holes at the bottom of the container, Jonathan and Lucy added a few rocks and filled the container with potting mix.

Lucy placed a miniature house in the garden.

Lucy loved Crassula ovata *'Ogre's Ears'.*

Glass pebbles make a perfect pond.

They added other miniature items to the fairy garden.

Watering the plants was the final task.

INDOOR ACTIVITIES

If you live in an area that experiences seasonal temperature changes, here are ten indoor gardening activities that will keep children interested through the winter weather. They will be excited watching nature in action indoors while everything outdoors is tucked up for the winter.

Construct a Rain Gauge

When using a rain gauge, children learn basic science skills such as recording data, weather patterns, and how to measure precipitation.

MATERIALS: A plastic bottle (2-liter soda bottle, 20-ounce [591 ml] soda bottle, or 16-ounce [480 ml] water bottle), a ruler, a piece of string about 14 inches (35.5 cm) long, adhesive tape, a permanent marker, and a handful of marbles, pebbles, or gravel.

METHOD: Cut off the top of the plastic bottle with a knife or scissors before handing it to your child. Have the child put the marbles, pebbles, or gravel in the bottom of the bottle to keep it from toppling over. Ask the child to use a ruler and a magic marker to mark 0 through 12 inches (0 through 30.5 cm) on the string. Show the child how to tape the string to the bottle so the 0-inch mark is at the top of the rocks. With a permanent marker, mark the inches (cm) on the bottle next to the marks on the string. Remove the string. The child may decorate the bottle with the permanent marker. (Any other marker or crayon will wash away when it rains.)

Place the gauge on a flat surface outside to collect the rain.

Have the child go outside frequently to check where the water line is and graph the results in a notebook or on a chart. Unlike glass, the plastic gauge will withstand some frozen water.

Create a Miniature Desert

Cultivate an indoor garden on a sunny windowsill with plants that do well inside in winter. A south- or west-facing window is an excellent place to try a succulent garden.

MATERIALS: A container, landscape fabric, potting mix formulated for cacti, a variety of succulents without thorns or bristles. *Echeveria* species are a good choice, but you can also try a jade plant (*Crassula* spp.).

METHOD: Choose a low container that has drainage holes. Cover the holes with landscape fabric. Have your child fill the container with a potting mix formulated for cacti, then add plants and rocks. Teach your child to be careful not to overwater the plants; if the soil feels moist, it does not need watering.

Children may be more willing to try new flavors from herbs they grow in their windowsill herb garden.

Plant a Windowsill Herb Garden

Herbs are an excellent choice for south-facing windowsills. You don't have to purchase an herb garden kit; you can grow herbs in small butter tubs or a colorful pot.

MATERIALS: A leftover container (if it does not have drainage holes, add them); craft materials such as paper, craft jewels, and yarn for decorating the container; landscape fabric, a soilless growing mix, herb seeds such as basil, chives, or parsley.

METHOD: Have the child decorate the container. Cover the drainage hole in the decorated container with landscape fabric. Fill it with the soilless growing mix. Help your child sow the herb seeds following the directions on the seed packet. When they are ready to harvest, involve your child in trimming the herbs. They may not be able to cut them, but they can hold a container for you to put the cuttings in. Children may be more willing to try new flavors using their windowsill herb garden's harvest.

Make a Terrarium

A terrarium is another type of indoor garden. It is a miniature garden grown in a covered glass or plastic container. You may buy a glass or acrylic terrarium (found easily online) or use a household container.

MATERIALS: A purchased terrarium or an old mayonnaise jar or a fishbowl; a soilless growing mix; charcoal (optional); small indoor or tropical plants; small objects like animal figurines; perlite if needed; and clear plastic wrap.

Setting up a terrarium can be an enjoyable activity for a child.

Paperwhites will grow happily and bloom with nothing more than water and stones or pebbles.

METHOD: Clean the container using soapy water and rinse it well. The child should fill the container with moist (not wet) potting mix to about one-half full, allowing enough room for plant roots. I like to add charcoal to the soil to help remove odors, but this is optional. Add the plants. The best ones are small, slow-growing, and perform well in humid environments, such as small ferns, miniature begonias, miniature African violets, and baby's tears (*Soleirolia*). Miniature begonias like the humidity but don't like wet feet, so add perlite to the growing mix. The child can be creative and arrange small objects to make a miniature landscape. Cover the terrarium with plastic and put it on a windowsill with indirect lighting. Do not place it in strong, direct sunlight.

Observe the terrarium closely for the first few days to check the moisture level. When in bright light, the sides and cover should become misty with water droplets.

Force Bulbs to Bloom

Paperwhites (*Narcissus*) will grow happily and bloom with nothing more than water and stones or pebbles. Children enjoy watching the roots grow.

MATERIALS: Paperwhite bulbs (find them at your local garden center, big box store, or online), a glass vase or bowl, stones or pebbles, three bamboo stakes, and twine.

METHOD: Have the child place a 2-inch (5 cm) layer of stones or pebbles in the bottom of a small vase, or about 4 inches (10 cm) in a larger container. The child should arrange the paperwhite bulbs close together on top of the stones with the roots facing down and the pointed part up. Put a few small rocks or pebbles around and between the bulbs to anchor them, exposing the tops. Add water until the level reaches just below the base of the bulbs. If the bulbs sit in water, they will rot. Place the container in a cool place away from direct heat.

Remind the child to check frequently and add water when the level falls 1 inch (2.5 cm) below the surface of the stones. After about three weeks, when your child sees the roots are well developed, move the container to a sunny window. Paperwhites tend to topple when they bloom; support them with bamboo stakes and twine when the shoots are about 8 inches (20 cm) tall. After the paperwhites finish blooming, toss them on the compost pile because they will not bloom again indoors.

Sprout Seeds

There are two ways to watch seeds sprout: using one type of seed in a jar or a variety of seeds in a simple mini greenhouse.

MATERIALS FOR THE FIRST METHOD: A glass jar with a lid, paper towels, and several seeds, such as zucchini or bush beans.

METHOD: Line the glass jar with a damp paper towel and put seeds between the glass and the towel. Attach the lid and leave the jar on the kitchen counter. Check the paper towel each day and moisten it as necessary. Your seeds should sprout in a few days.

MATERIALS FOR THE SECOND METHOD: A recycled aluminum foil pan, a paper towel, seeds such as zucchini, scarlet runner beans, cucumbers, and broccoli, and a plastic bag big enough to hold the pan.

METHOD: Position a damp paper towel in the bottom of the pan and gently place the seeds on it. Your child may put several of each in rows. Draw a simple map showing where the child placed each seed variety so it's easy to identify which seeds sprout first. Encourage the child to make predictions. Put the tray in a plastic bag. Once the seeds and roots grow, you may talk about germination and how different seeds have different germination periods. I am always amazed at how quickly the tray explodes with sprouted seeds and plants.

Care for Houseplants

Caring for a plant is a valuable activity for children of all ages as they learn responsibility and the satisfaction of nurturing a living thing.

MATERIALS: Choose hardy houseplants, like pothos, that increase quickly and do not need much light, a plant mister (sprayer), a sponge, snippers, small pots, a soilless growing mix, and a magnifying glass.

METHOD: Take children to a garden center or big box store and let each select a plant, avoiding sharp, prickly, or toxic plants. Preschoolers can mist leaves with a sprayer and use a sponge to clean dusty leaves. When I visited my family in Arizona, I encouraged my grandson Anthony to help

A hardy houseplant like pothos is easy for a child to grow.

Venus flytraps excite the imagination.

remove dead leaves from some bedraggled-looking potted plants. He took the responsibility seriously and did a good job. Show them how to pot the off-shoots of spider plants (spiderettes), which form on the ends of the runners. In time, the offshoots will root and you will have a new houseplant to enjoy.

Randy Seagraves, program specialist for the Junior Master Gardener Program at Texas A&M University, suggests providing children with a magnifying glass to detect why a plant failed to thrive. Tell them to look for clues to determine what the plant might need using the acronym PLANTS: place, light, air, nutrients, thirst (water), and soil. They will learn many lessons and skills they can transfer to growing outdoor plants.

Grow a Venus Flytrap

Insect-eating plants excite a child's imagination. I found this was true with Anthony's brother, Mateo, who showed little interest in gardening until I asked him if he wanted to own a Venus flytrap (*Dionaea muscipula*). He said, "I think it will be fun." Venus flytrap is a small bog plant native to the Carolinas. The leaves are specifically designed to trap soft-bodied insects. The plant digests the trapped insect in about a week, then reopens.

MATERIALS: A Venus flytrap plant, terrarium, planting medium, and distilled water. Mateo was excited to receive a Venus flytrap that I purchased online. You can buy one at some local garden centers.

METHOD: Venus flytrap grows in a sunny, cool area with high humidity; a terrarium is ideal. I sent a small terrarium and planting medium along with the plant and instructions to Mateo. The planting medium comprised about 65 percent sphagnum moss and 35 percent sand. I could not be there to help Mateo plant his new acquisition, but he did a great job following instructions. He put the planting medium in the terrarium, removed the Venus flytrap from the plant pot, and planted it in the planting medium. I told him to water with distilled water and keep the planting medium moist but not overly wet.

Do not fertilize the Venus flytrap as you feed it by releasing small flies inside the terrarium. The insects must be alive. The plant can go long periods, however, without eating insects. They do not like drought, fertilization, or low humidity. They also dislike tampering with the traps too much. Who can resist this intriguing plant?

A bog garden is on my bucket list, where I will grow Venus flytraps. Venus flytrap is winter hardy to USDA zones 7 through 10, but with adequate winter protection it may also survive winters in USDA zones 5 and 6.

Compost with Worms

Worm composting, or vermicomposting, uses worms to recycle food scraps and other organic material into a valuable soil amendment. This activity will produce incredible nutrients for your garden.

MATERIALS: A shallow plastic or wooden 5- to 10-gallon (19 to 38 l) container, a plastic bag or sheet of plastic if the container is made of wood, moist strips of newspaper, garden soil, compost or shredded leaves, red worms or red wigglers purchased online from a worm farm, and kitchen scraps.

METHOD: Rinse out the container and put plastic on the bottom if it is made of wood. Add bedding made of newspaper strips or leaves. Fill the box with soil, organic matter such as compost or shredded leaves, and a few worms. Cover the bin with a loose-fitting lid that allows air to circulate. Keep it moist and in a shady spot.

The child adds kitchen scraps, preferably raw fruit and vegetables (except for broccoli, citrus fruits, onions, and orange rinds). In a favorable environment, your worms will work tirelessly to produce compost. It is an easy, fun way for children to learn the importance of composting, discover the value of worms, and learn about the interdependence of plants and organisms.

Grow a Garbage Garden

Children love that they can grow a collection of houseplants using only kitchen garbage.

MATERIALS: The tops of root crops such as beets, carrots, or turnips; the seed from a ripe avocado; seeds from citrus fruits; pie plate; pebbles; a container and potting mix for the avocado seed.

METHOD: Create a leafy garden by placing the tops of root crops on pebbles covered in water on a pie plate. Roots and feathery leaves will soon develop. The child can grow an avocado plant by removing the seed from a ripe avocado and planting it in a 6-inch (15.2 cm) container of potting mix. Try planting the seeds from citrus fruits, first soaking

The top of a root vegetable growing in water.

> them in warm water for six to twelve hours. Garbage gardening shows children there is value in many things we throw away.

Other excellent winter gardening activities for children include making a bird feeder by cutting a bagel in half, spreading it with cooking fat, dredging it with birdseed, and hanging it in the yard; reading children's books like *The Tale of Peter Rabbit* or *The Secret Garden*; and pouring over seed catalogs to plan next season's garden.

Children will learn valuable gardening principles and have fun doing whichever activities you choose. We must use positive strategies as we teach children to care for our fantastic environment and encourage them to look for solutions to today's problems. Doug Tallamy, in his 2023 book *Nature's Best Hope: Young Readers' Edition* (Timber Press), explains to middle school children that they can be proactive and make a difference. With help and encouragement from us, our children, as ambassadors to the future, give us hope for solving the multiple environmental problems of today, leading to a better tomorrow.

Epilogue

Gardening in the Pocono Mountains, where I live, is fraught with difficulties—from rock-hard ground to marauding deer that believe I planted a buffet just for them. In addition to these concerns, the enormous contemporary challenges I outline in this book may make you wonder why I choose to garden. I garden because I have discovered that my cottage garden provides an opportunity to learn and implement solutions to these seemingly insurmountable problems. As gardeners, there is much we can do—from being mindful of our energy consumption to growing plants native to the area, gardening sustainably, and creating a garden that pollinators will relish. As you employ good gardening practices, especially growing the right plant in the right place, you will make a garden to live in, a place where you can enjoy the beauty of nature, experience feelings of accomplishment, and take pride in your contributions to and respect for the environment. And you can do this if you have a large expanse, a balcony, or even a windowsill for a few pots.

I am so proud of my garden's appearance of uncontrived beauty, its productive kitchen garden, the effective rain garden, and a delightful meadow humming with pollinators. The beauty of my garden is a constant source of inspiration and motivation for me. I enjoy sharing my garden with others as I have done throughout the pages of this book. This love for my garden gives me feelings of contentment and hope, and I believe it can inspire you, too.

Of course, it took time to create the many elements of my garden. If you are a beginning gardener, it may seem overwhelming. Your challenge is to identify the global issues most affecting your garden and those most concerning to you and tackle them one at a time. Begin slowly; begin small. First, set one or two manageable goals, such as planting something for bees and pollinators, planting an extra row of vegetables for sharing, or starting a compost pile. My goals were more ambitious so I put them into a five-year plan. I determined how much I could do in one gardening season (and how much I could afford) and spread the main tasks over the five years: one year, a rain garden, another a meadow, for example.

Try not to overthink your plan, and be flexible—your plan is not cast in stone, and you may change it at any time. An essential characteristic of cottage garden design is that no two cottage gardens are the same. Your garden will reflect your tastes and ideas as you create new memories in your beautiful space.

Finally, we have hope through the young, future gardeners we nurture. Sharing with them what we learn about preserving our environment is a beautiful legacy we can leave. It is a responsibility we all share, and by nurturing the next generation of gardeners, we can ensure a sustainable future for our planet. The miracle of watching a tiny seed develop into a thriving plant is a wonderful reminder that even small efforts can result in major accomplishments: a beacon of hope for gardeners as we navigate the environmental challenges before us.

References

AmpleHarvest.org. "AmpleHarvest.org in Indian Country." May 20, 2022. ampleharvest.org/inindiancountry.

Balagtas, Joseph. "Economic Gloom: Making Sense of the Confusion Over the State of the Economy." *Chew on This!* Blog Series. Purdue University College of Agriculture. December 8, 2023. ag.purdue.edu/cfdas/chew-on-this/economic-gloom-making-sense-of-the-confusion-over-the-state-of-the-economy.

Bartholomew, Mel. *All New Square Foot Gardening: Grow More in Less Space!* Minneapolis: Cool Springs Press, 2006.

Bartholomew, Mel. *Square Metre Gardening: The Radical Approach to Gardening That Really Works*. London: Francis Lincoln, 2013.

Blanusa, Tijana. "Gardens and Cooling: The Importance of Plant Choice." Royal Horticultural Society. December 31, 2015. rhs.org.uk/science/gardening-in-a-changing-world/environmental-projects/plants-and-aerial-cooling.

Burdett, James H. *The Victory Garden Manual*. Chicago: Ziff-Davis, 1943.

Carson, Rachel. *Silent Spring*. Boston: Houghton Mifflin, 2002.

Chatto, Beth, and Christopher Lloyd. *Dear Friend and Gardener: Letters on Life and Gardening*. London: Frances Lincoln, 1998.

Chicago Botanic Garden. "Rain Gardens." 2024. chicagobotanic.org/conservation/rain_garden.

Clarke, Ethne, and Clay Perry. *English Country Gardens*. Paperback edition. Broadwell, Oxfordshire: Cassell and Company, 2000.

Cornell College of Agriculture and Life Sciences Garden-Based Learning. *Gardening in Our Warming World: Youth Grow!* 2024. gardening.cals.cornell.edu/lessons/gardening-in-our-warming-world-youth-grow.

Donley, Nathan. "How the EPA's Lax Regulation of Dangerous Pesticides Is Hurting Public Health and the US Economy." *Brookings Institution Economic Studies Bulletin*. September 29, 2022. brookings.edu/articles/how-the-epas-lax-regulation-of-dangerous-pesticides-is-hurting-public-health-and-the-us-economy.

Drake, Olivia. "Looks Matter: New Research Reveals Which Houseplants Are Best for Well-Being." Royal Horticultural Society. n.d. rhs.org.uk/science/articles/houseplants-for-wellbeing.

Eddison, Sydney. *Gardening for a Lifetime: How to Garden Wiser as You Grow Older*. Portland, OR: Timber Press, 2010.

Ellis, Lauren, Fiona Mathews, and Max Anderson. "Moths Are More Efficient Pollinators than Bees, Shows New Research." University of Sussex. March 30, 2023. sussex.ac.uk/broadcast/read/60568.

Environmental Protection Agency. "Criteria Air Pollutants." October 22, 2024. epa.gov/criteria-air-pollutants.

Environmental Protection Agency. "Urbanization and Stormwater Runoff." February 7, 2024. epa.gov/sourcewaterprotection/urbanization-and-stormwater-runoff.

Environmental Protection Agency. "Wildfires." March 14, 2024. epa.gov/natural-disasters/wildfires.

Feeding America. "Bill Emerson Act." October 1, 1996. feedingamerica.org/ways-to-give/corporate-and-foundations/product-partner/bill-emerson.

Fernando, Nimali, and Melanie Potock. "Gardening with Kids: How It Affects Your Child's Brain, Body, and Soul." Public Broadcasting Service. March 16, 2016. pbs.org/parents/thrive/gardening-with-kids-how-it-affects-your-childs-brain-body-and-soul.

Ferrari, Olivia. "Streetlights Are Influencing Nature—From How Leaves Grow to How Insects Eat." *National Geographic*. August 5, 2024. nationalgeographic.com/environment/article/artificial-night-sky-light-pollution-trees-insects.

Goodall, Jane. "What We Do." Jane Goodall Institute of Canada. 2024. janegoodall.ca/what-we-do.

Homegrown National Park. "About Us." 2024. homegrownnationalpark.org/about-us.

John F. Kennedy Presidential Library and Museum. "Remarks of Senator John F. Kennedy, Convocation of the United Negro College Fund, Indianapolis, Indiana, April 12, 1959." jfklibrary.org/archives/other-resources/john-f-kennedy-speeches/indianapolis-in-19590412.

Jones, Charisse. "Does Remote Work Increase Anxiety? For Parents, Work from Home May Hurt Mental Health." *USA Today*. Updated June 11, 2024. usatoday.com/story/money/2023/05/15/remote-work-mental-health-toll-parents/70208895007.

Molinari, Nicolas, and Rachel Ledbetter. "How Summertime Fun Is Brought to You By American Business." US Chamber of Commerce. July 1, 2024. uschamber.com/economy/how-summertime-fun-is-brought-to-you-by-american-business.

National Oceanic and Atmospheric Administration. "International Report Confirms Record-High Global Temperatures, Greenhouse Gases in 2023." August 22, 2024. noaa.gov/news-release/international-report-confirms-record-high-global-temperatures-greenhouse-gases-in-2023.

Paz-Ferreiro, Jorge, Aurora Nieto, Ana Méndez, Matthew Peter James Askeland, and Gabriel Gascó. "Biochar from Biosolids Pyrolysis: A Review." *International Journal of Environmental Research and Public Health* 15, no. 5 (May 10, 2018): 956. doi.org/10.3390/ijerph15050956.

Pennsylvania Horticultural Society. "Community Gardens." 2023. phsonline.org/programs/community-gardens#:~:text=Philadelphia%20is%20the%20poorest%20big%20city%20in,together%20to%20build%20social%20connections%20and%20community.

Raček, Jakub, Jan Sevcik, Tomáš Chorazy, Jiri Kucerik, and Petr Hlavinek. "Biochar—Recovery Material from Pyrolysis of Sewage Sludge: A Review." *Waste and Biomass Valorization* 11 (April 20, 2019): 3677–3709. doi.org/10.1007/s12649-019-00679-w.

Ray, Robbin. "How Low Can You Mow? Lazy Lawn-mowing Can Be Better for the Environment." University of New Hampshire UNH Today. June 1, 2022. unh.edu/unhtoday/2022/06/how-low-can-you-mow.

Royal Horticultural Society. "Writer, broadcaster, gardener and farmer, Monty Don has backed our exciting new collaboration with the NHS . . ." February 27, 2018. Facebook. facebook.com/rhshome/posts/writer-broadcaster-gardener-and-farmer-monty-don-has-backed-our-exciting-new-col/10155303559191220.

Royal Horticultural Society Science. "Greener Gardens Promote Healthier Residents." October 6, 2020. rhs.org.uk/advice/health-and-wellbeing/articles/greener-gardens-promote-healthier-residents.

Sandborn, Dixie. "Nature Smart—Part 1." Michigan State University. January 31, 2013. canr.msu.edu/news/nature_smart_part_1.

Stoecklin, Vicki. "Developmentally Appropriate Gardening for Young Children." White Hutchinson Leisure & Learning Group. (n.d.) whitehutchinson.com/children/articles/gardening.shtml.

Tallamy, Douglas W. *Nature's Best Hope: A New Approach to Conservation That Starts in Your Yard*. Portland, OR: Timber Press, 2019.

Tallamy, Douglas W. *Nature's Best Hope (Young Readers' Edition): How You Can Save the World in Your Own Yard*. Portland, OR: Timber Press, 2023.

Turner, Charlotte. *Beachy Head: With Other Poems*. London: J. Johnson, 1807.

United States Department of Agriculture. "Climate Change Adaptation." 2024. usda.gov/oce/energy-and-environment/climate/adaptation#plan.

Vogt, Benjamin. *Prairie Up: An Introduction to Natural Garden Design*. Champaign, IL: University of Illinois Press, 2023.

Washington State University. "Rural Stormwater Solutions: Managing Water." 2024. ruralstormwater.wsu.edu/options-for-managing-water.

World Health Organization. "COVID-19 Pandemic Triggers 25% Increase in Prevalence of Anxiety and Depression Worldwide." March 2, 2022. who.int/news/item/02-03-2022-covid-19-pandemic-triggers-25-increase-in-prevalence-of-anxiety-and-depression-worldwide.

Acknowledgments

It is a great honor to have the opportunity to write this book, and I am deeply grateful to Timber Press for entrusting me with this project and for the vision and guidance of my editors. I signed up with GardenComm, an organization of garden communicators, for a "Pitch the Editors" session—this made everything possible, for which I thank this wonderful organization.

I will always be grateful to Linda Wiles, Penn State Extension educator, for teaching me how gardening in the United States differs from England, and to Nancy Knauss, Statewide Master Gardener Coordinator, for proofreading my newspaper articles for many years and significantly honing my garden writing.

One of my biggest challenges was keeping my garden photo-ready while meeting writing deadlines. I want to express my sincere thanks to the master gardeners of Monroe County for answering my call for help in the garden during a tough time.

The sacrifices and understanding of my family and friends throughout the writing process, often at the expense of our personal time together, are deeply appreciated. I am truly blessed to have the unwavering support and help of my husband, Duane, and my grandson Jonathan. Jonathan has helped me in the garden since he could walk. I am also thankful for Jenny Rose Carey's support. Her countless helpful acts and words of encouragement have been a constant source of inspiration.

I am indebted to my dear friends, Janet Tate, my proofreader, and Rob Cardillo, my photographer. Janet read every word, and her advice made this book much better. I can never repay her hours of dedication to this venture. Rob's brilliant photography enhanced the book beyond measure. His unwavering patience, kindness, and friendship helped me navigate this project every step of the way.

Finally, I draw inspiration from my young friend Lucy. Her infectious joy of gardening gives me hope for a brighter future. Lucy is a testament to the positive impact young people can have on the environment and on our world.

Photography Credits

All photographs are by the author or photographer except the following:

Christine Gresh, 199

Janet Tate, 188 (bottom), 215, 221

Jenny Rose Carey, 23

Meredith Ward, 191

Samantha Thorpe, 82

Shutterstock, 45 (left), 123 (left), 132, 144 (right), 159, 168 (bottom), 230

Garden designs, as follows:

Linda Allard, 128 (right)

The Met Cloisters, 158

Michael Lizotte, 5, 56–57

Robinson Anderson and Summers, 162 (top)

Index

Photo: Susie Forrester

PAMELA HUBBARD, with more than twenty years of experience as a speaker, educator, and writer, is a trusted source of tips and advice for the home gardener on all garden- and plant-related issues. Her expertise makes her a sought-after speaker for nationwide garden clubs, flower shows, and horticultural groups. Pam writes an award-winning blog, and her monthly newspaper article, Gardening in the Poconos, earned a GardenComm silver medal. As a master gardener emeritus, she is often called upon to train new master gardeners for Penn State Extension. Pam was born in England and acquired her love of gardening at her grandmother's knee. Her gardens have received three blue ribbons from the Pennsylvania Horticultural Society and have been featured in *Country Gardens* magazine. You can find her endlessly pursuing her dream of re-creating her grandmother's cottage garden at Astolat Farm in the Pocono Mountains of Pennsylvania, where she lives with her husband and two adorable goats named Doodles and Petunia.